WORLD ATLAS
OF SUSTAINABLE DEVELOPMENT

Éditions Autrement

Autrement would like to thank Cécile Mazzacurati, Silvia Ritossa and Anne Bailly
for their support and expertise.
Director: *Henry Dougier*
Managing editor: *Laure Flavigny, Bertrand Richard*
Press and medias: *Emmanuelle Savy*
Layout and maps:
Cartographic director: Anne Bailly
AEBK, cartes et communication, 8 rue Eugène-Varlin 75010 Paris
with Lenny Dollé, Lorena Farias-Deschanel, Michel Raymonenq,
Thanks to Jacques Bertin for the planisphere and Mémorial de Caen for the spread "desertification"
English translator: *Carmela Uranga*
Consultant: *John Monteville Smith, consultant for ernvironmental publications*
Proof reader: *Elisabeth Leighton-Jones*

aebk

© Éditions Autrement 2002
77, rue du Faubourg-Saint-Antoine, 75011 Paris
tel : (331) 44 73 80 00 - fax : (331) 44 73 00 12
www.autrement.com

ISSN: 1272-0151
ISBN : 2-7467-0290-8

WORLD ATLAS
OF SUSTAINABLE DEVELOPMENT

Anne-Marie Sacquet

Éditions Autrement - Atlas/World

autrement

Acknowledgements

Anne-Marie Sacquet would like to thank the members of the editorial committee for their enlightened assistance, as well as the NGOs - Transparency, Médecins sans Frontières, Reporters sans Frontières, Plan Bleu (Jean Margat) - that produced, supplied and validated precious and often unpublished data. Special thanks to Silvia Ritossa, Ben Cramer and Patrick Legrand for their expertise and support, and to Serge Antoine for his stimulating collaboration.

Le Comité 21

Le Comité 21, a French committee concerned with sustainable development and the environment, was created in 1994 following commitments France made at Rio regarding implementation of Agenda 21. Its nearly 300 members are organized into four groups representative of civil society: business, regional authorities, associations, and public institutions. The mission of Le Comité 21 is to make recommendations for sustainable development - in areas such as Local Agenda 21s, sustainable development initiatives in enterprises, international cooperation to meet basic needs, participation by all stakeholders - and disseminate these recommendations.

Author: Anne-Marie Sacquet, supervising director

Scientific coordination: Silvia Ritossa, responsible for international cooperation

Communication-diffusion: Marie Bernard, Christine Delhaye, Claire Sehier.

Editorial Committee

Under the patronage of the United Nations Environment Programme (UNEP)

PNUE

President : Serge Antoine, Honorary President of Le Comité 21, member of the Mediterranean Commission on Sustainable Development (MCSD), United Nations Special Adviser for the Earth Summit at Rio

- Jacqueline Aloisi de Larderel, Assistant Executive Director, UNEP

- Christian Averous, Organisation for Co-operation and Economic Development (OCED)

- Alain Chosson, Consommation logement et cadre de vie (CLCV)

CLCV
CONSOMMATION
LOGEMENT ET
CADRE DE VIE

- Ben Cramer, Radio France Internationale (RFI)

- Thierry Lavoux, French Institute for the Environment (IFEN)

- Thierry Thouvenot, World Wildlife Fund (WWF)

- Michel Mousel, President, French Committee for the World Summit on Sustainable Development (CFSMDD)

WWF

- Ronan Uhel, European Environment Agency (EEA)

European Environment Agency

Sources

Amnesty International
Australian Institute of Marine Science
CIA (US Central Intelligence Agency)
CRED (Centre for Research on the Epidemiology of Disasters)
Dow Jones Sustainability Index
EIA (US Energy Information Administration)
FAO (UN Food and Agricultural Organization)
IEA (International Energy Agency)
IISS (International Institute for Strategic Studies)
ILO (International Labour Organisation)
Internet Software Consortium
IPU (Inter-Parliamentary Union)
IRIS (Institut des relations internationales et stratégiques)
ISAAA (International Service for the Acquisition of Agri-biotech Applications)
ITOPF (International Tanker Owners Pollution Federation)
ITU (International Telecommunication Union)
IUCN (World Conservation Union)
Max Havelaar Association

Médecins sans frontières (Doctors without Borders)
OECD (Organisation for Economic Co-operation and Economic Development)
Population Reference Bureau
Red Cross, World Disasters Report 2001
Reporters sans frontières (Reporters without Borders)
SIPRI (Stockholm International Peace Research Institute)
Terranova
Transparency International
UN (United Nations)
UNAIDS
UNEP (United Nations Environment Programme)
UNESCO (United Nations Educational, Scientific and Cultural Organization)
UNICEF (United Nations Children's Fund)
WHO (World Health Organization)
The World Bank
World Resources Institute
WWF (World Wildlife Fund)

Contents

Sustainable development:
where concerns for social welfare and the environment intersect

"Let us be brothers, not so that we can be saved, but because we are lost."
Edgar Morin, Anne-Brigitte Kern, Terre-Patrie , Seuil/FNAC, 1993

"Poverty is the greatest cause of pollution."
Indira Gandhi

In June 1992, at the first Earth Summit organized by the United Nations, the term "sustainable development" was at the centre of all discussions. 170 heads of state and government agreed an action programme for the 21st century - Agenda 21 - which defined a set of objectives for the planet's sustainable development . The summit mobilized institutions, scientists, NGOs, indigenous peoples, business and "citizens of the world" during a two-week period. Over 9,000 journalists covered this event. Aspirations for a new kind of world - more just, safer, and more respectful of human beings and the environment - began to emerge.

This extraordinary gathering arose from a sense of urgency provoked by the depletion of the Earth's resources, the increasing number of natural disasters, and the exclusion of a large share of humanity. The means used up until then to stimulate growth, based on immediate profits for a small minority, had resulted in a deadlock. Sustainable development heralded a well-controlled form of growth, capable of meeting the needs of the world's people while preserving ecological, social and economic stability in the long term as well as the short term.

Sustainability is only possible if certain goals are adopted: our planet should become more just, in that poverty and inequality should no longer be acceptable; all its inhabitants should have the right to live, not merely to survive; and it should be viable, providing basic necessities for all without any compromises in terms of providing for future generations.

Agenda 21, agreed by the governments represented at Rio, called for greater interaction between human activities: maintenance of ecosystems, economic efficiency and the balance of social systems. It addressed the urgent need to fight poverty, to establish equitable regulations governing international trade, and to introduce the precautionary principle with respect to environmental protection. The central issue of all the discussions at Rio was the need to introduce the notion of human dignity into decision-making (accessibility to basic necessities, protection of human rights, recognition of the role of NGOs). A new form of governance was proposed, founded on concepts of responsibility, the preservation of stability, and citizens' participation in decision-making that affects the present and future.

What is the situation in 2002? The Earth Summit criticized existing trends, but has it been possible to reverse them? Unfortunately, the general assessment today is that the expectations raised at Rio have not been fulfilled.

The "change of tack" advocated at Rio was intended to lead to radical changes in the very concept of development, and therefore in existing modes of production and distribution of wealth. Ten years on, it is clear that such changes are not taking place. We are still in the eye of the storm: modes of production and consumption continue to endanger health and the environment – and often the signs can only be recognized on a long-term basis and therefore too late. We give priority to responses to existing pollution rather than pollution prevention. We consume resources that should be safeguarded for future generations while degrading our own living conditions.

Regarding social welfare, things are not going much better. The gulf between lifestyles is still increasing; poverty, exclusion and violence affect many of the largest cities both the North and South. Industrialized countries continue to profit from the mining, agricultural and forest resources of developing countries. Inequality is intolerable from the point of view of our common humanity, and in the long term it threatens social and economic structures. By the year 2050, 85% of the world population will live in countries that are said to be "developing" today. If not on a humane level, then on a realistic one, we should perhaps begin to envisage that such a population might eventually refuse to accept domination by a minority of countries whose economic and technological approaches have already shown their limitations.

Neither political and economic leaders nor international institutions have been able to provide adequate responses to the challenges posed by the international community at Rio. Inertia within institutions, lack of political will, and an attitude of supremacy in North-South relations have resulted in a series of partial measures that are inadequate to arrest social and environmental damage.

The dominating powers can be compared to a giant figure made of clay beginning to feel the earth crumble at its feet. A number of warning signs - political (Southern countries increasingly refuse to accept the North's authoritarianism), climatic (the 1999 natural disasters) or economic (the bankruptcy of several American "success stories") - remind us of our fragility and that of existing systems.

The question now is how to respond - or rather, what questions to ask. Thus this Atlas proposes a "radioscopy" of the planet from a variety of viewpoints that cannot be disassociated. Is sustainable management of tropical forests possible if people in producer countries do not have the means to survive? Can poverty be combatted effectively without first and definitively solving the problem of external debt? How can millions of children be saved from health problems related to contaminated water if access to safe water is not recognized globally as a human right? Can there be progress in the struggle against corruption if freedom of speech is not ensured worldwide?

A new approach to development is required - one capable of tackling these issues from every angle. This approach should be more responsible, more transparent and more humane. We are interdependent and fragile, and therefore we should have a greater sense of solidarity. The solutions that will give us hope that another world is possible are already in the process of being outlined by individuals who have not as yet taken centre stage.

A word to the reader:

Reality is often well-concealed: for example, the extreme poverty existing in Northern countries or the environmental impacts of armed conflicts. Lack of adequate data shows that progress still needs to be made with respect to transparency of information. For this reason some of the maps should be interpreted with a certain degree of caution (e.g. where legends indicate that there are "no data available"). An attempt has been made to reconcile exactitude and concision. Thus the Atlas should not be considered to present a comprehensive overview of themes (the 30 proposed seem unavoidable) or a comprehensive analysis (only urban transport is treated in the Transport section, though there is much to be said about transport by air and goods transport). Finally, it is only through juxtaposing facts and figures, and comparing the maps, that the data can reveal their real significance. An interactive reading is therefore recommended (see the index).

If you have any suggestions, send them to: atlas@comite21.org

International conventions

Since its creation in 1945, the United Nations has brought over 500 international Conventions into operation. Each Convention, whether it applies to children's rights or the protection of the planet's oceans, has to be signed, ratified and put into practice by signatory States. Every Convention is an obstacle course.

Such Conventions often manage to highlight a previously marginalized or well-concealed question, such as the 1995 Beijing Convention on the status of women. If a lot still needs to be done, since this symbolic assembly at least women now have the right to free speech in the majority of countries.

However, Conventions are often still waiting to be ratified by a large number of countries before the problems can be fully tackled. The United States is the principal consumer of the planet's resources, yet it has refused to ratify the Convention on Biodiversity, which was developed following the Rio Earth Summit, or the 1997 Kyoto Protocol, which called for application of the Climate Change Convention and reduction of greenhouse gases.

Some progress has nevertheless been made. In 1993 the Basel Convention prohibited OECD countries from exporting toxic waste to other countries, and in 2001 over 10 years of negotiations led to a Convention being adopted in Stockholm aiming at eliminating persistent organic pollutants (POPs)!

Many international organizations and NGOs are calling for greater coherence between Conventions and complaining that UN structures continue to function on the basis of outdated notions of "North and South". Northern countries, having undermined the South's cultures and resources, now talk about how to save the world. Governments in many developing coun-

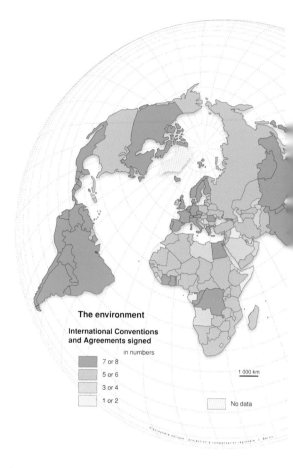

The environment

International Conventions and Agreements signed

in numbers

- 7 or 8
- 5 or 6
- 3 or 4
- 1 or 2
- No data

1 000 km

tries are beginning to claim the right to act for themselves.

In today's world there no organization is capable of arbitrating or settling conflict. Only the World Trade Organization has access to such power. Shouldn't human rights and the environment deserve more?

Sources: FAO, UN

Several hundred United Nations Conventions are in the process of being ratified

Find out more

Japan ratified the Kyoto Protocol in June 2002.

The Environment

Eight Conventions are represented in this map, which shows when they were ratified: the Convention on Biodiversity (adopted in 1992) and the Kyoto Protocol (1997), the Convention against Desertification (adopted in 1994), the Convention for the Conservation of Humid Zones (adopted in 1975 at Ramsar), the Convention against the Trade of Endangered Species (Cites, adopted in 1975), the Convention for the Conservation of World Heritage (1972), and the International Agreement on Tropical Wood (adopted in 1994).

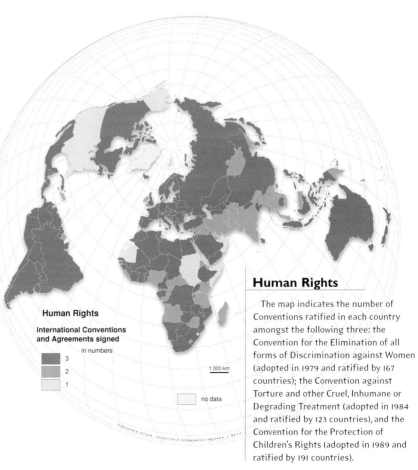

Human Rights

International Conventions and Agreements signed
in numbers

- 3
- 2
- 1

no data

1 000 km

Human Rights

The map indicates the number of Conventions ratified in each country amongst the following three: the Convention for the Elimination of all forms of Discrimination against Women (adopted in 1979 and ratified by 167 countries); the Convention against Torture and other Cruel, Inhumane or Degrading Treatment (adopted in 1984 and ratified by 123 countries), and the Convention for the Protection of Children's Rights (adopted in 1989 and ratified by 191 countries).

9

Can we even begin to imagine a future for our
planet when the majority of its inhabitants now
suffer from hunger and repression? Human
development is one of the main objectives
of sustainable development. It implies respect
for human rights, physical and moral integrity,
and access to basic necessities: food, health care,
education, and participation in decisions that
affect the present and future.
The highest priorities are fighting poverty and
ending discrimination and conflicts, which lead to
human, environmental and economic degradation.

Human Development

Population growth rates

The global population increases by 1.3% per year. Reproduction rates are highest in poor countries, especially in some of the most densely populated ones. 50% of world population growth occurs in just six countries: India (21% of the total), China, Pakistan, Nigeria, Bangladesh and Indonesia.

According to United Nations estimates, by 2050 the planet's total population will increase by 50% (9.3 billion people compared with 6.1 billion in 2001). It is estimated that 85% of these people will live in what are considered developing countries today. These figures emphasise the importance of ensuring equitable relationships between the North and the South.

The inhabitants of many poor countries already have extreme difficulty obtaining basic necessities like food. The development process has an essential role to play, as demographic control goes hand in hand with the promotion of women's rights.

In developed countries, reproduction rates (1.6 children per woman) are below the renewal threshold (2.1). Thus the population as a whole is getting progressively older and it is up to the "active" population to finance existing pension schemes. In some countries, where there is little immigration, the total population may even begin to diminish.

Migration has developed to satisfy reciprocal interests: on the whole, immigrant workers have been filling jobs that the local population does not want. A whole economic system therefore develops, as immigrants transfer financial resources to their home countries. As immigrants intermingle with local populations, mutual tolerance and respect become of increasing importance.

Discrimination often occurs with respect to certain minority populations: in Hungary, for example, the life expectancy of the Roma (Gypsy) popu-lation is on average ten to fifteen

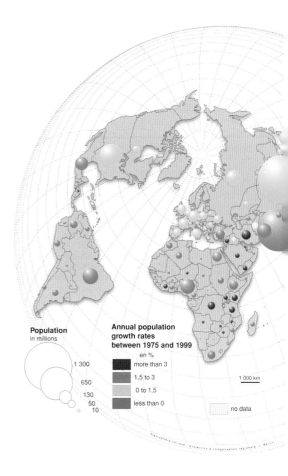

Population
in millions

1 300
650
130
50
10

Annual population growth rates
between 1975 and 1999

en %
more than 3
1,5 to 3
0 to 1,5
less than 0

1 000 km

no data

years shorter than that of the rest of the country.

Obviously, population movements are increasing throughout the world. Immigration is not just a Western phenomenon. It is therefore essential to address this issue in greater depth and with increased competence.

Life expectancy at birth

	Middle East and North Africa	South Asia	Latin America	East Asia and the Pacific	OECD	Europe et Central Asia	Sub-Saharan Africa
1990	68	63	70	69	78	69	47
	+9	+9	+5	+4	+4	+1	-1
1980	59	54	65	65	74	68	48

Sub-Saharan Africa is the only region in the world where life expectancy has fallen, and it was already very low. AIDS, with which over 23 million people have been infected, is one of the main causes.

Sources: World Bank, UN

demography

By 2050, 85% of the world population will live in today's developing countries.

Immigration/emigration

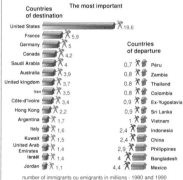

Countries of destination	The most important
United States	19,6
France	5,9
Germany	5
Canada	4,2
Saudi Arabia	4
Australia	3,9
United kingdom	3,7
Iran	3,5
Côte-d'Ivoire	3,4
Hong Kong	2,2
Argentina	1,7
Italy	1,6
Kuwait	1,5
United Arab Emirates	1,4
Israël	1,4
Jordan	1,1

Countries of departure

0,7	Péru
0,8	Zambia
0,8	Thailand
0,8	Colombia
0,9	Ex-Yugoslavia
0,9	Sri Lanka
1	Vietnam
2,4	Indonesia
2,4	China
2,9	Philippines
4	Bangladesh
4,4	Mexico

number of immigrants ou emigrants in millions - 1980 and 1990

The preferred destination of emigrants remains the United States, which has not received so many foreigners since the beginning of the 20th century.

Many people leave their homes in Mexico and Bangladesh, for example, to escape poverty.

Find out more

Global financial transfers by immigrant workers to their home countries have reached 70 billion dollars per year, surpassing total international development assistance.

➤ Status of Women
Corruption
International Solidarities

Population growth

The global population increases by 83 million every year. 99% of this growth occurs in the poorest countries of Africa, Asia, Latin America and the Caribbean, and Oceania.

Reproduction rates

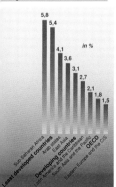

5,8
5,4
4,1
3,6
3,1
2,7
2,1
1,8
1,5

in %

Sub-Saharan Africa / Least developed countries / Arab States / East Asia / Developing countries / Latin America and the Caribbean / South Asia and the Pacific / OECD / Eastern Europe and the CIS

Reproduction rates are highest in poor countries, where there is the least access to adequate health care. Mortality rates for women during birth or pregnancy are also very high, while contraception is rare (less than 15% of couples).

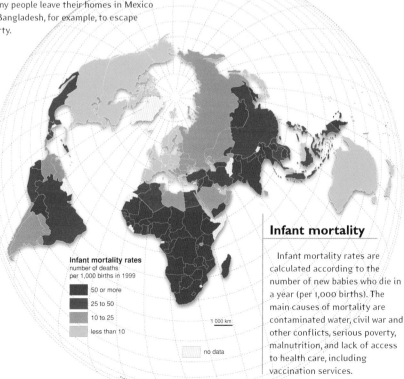

Infant mortality rates
number of deaths
per 1,000 births in 1999

- 50 or more
- 25 to 50
- 10 to 25
- less than 10

1 000 km

- no data

Infant mortality

Infant mortality rates are calculated according to the number of new babies who die in a year (per 1,000 births). The main causes of mortality are contaminated water, civil war and other conflicts, serious poverty, malnutrition, and lack of access to health care, including vaccination services.

Access to water

Water is essential for life. Humans need to consume an average of 1.5 litres of water per day. 10% water loss can cause hallucinations; 15% water loss results in certain death. We can die if deprived of water for four days, whereas it is possible to survive several weeks without food.

Water must be drinkable and accessible. 71% of the planet's surface area is water, but 97% of this water is too salty to drink. The remaining 3% of fresh water is largely groundwater or ice. Demand for fresh water is in fact met by 0.3% of total global water reserves.

There is great disparity in the worldwide distribution of this precious resource. Fewer than 10 countries possess 60% of available fresh water. Between countries as different as Iceland or the Golf Emirates, access to these resources per capita can vary by a factor of 1 to 20,000. Brazil, for example, has a total 5,670 km^3 of available fresh water per year and Malta just 25 km^3. Many of the world's arid regions experience fresh water shortages. "Water stress" can lead to conflict, for example in the Middle East.

Although water is a scarce resource, it is wasted, polluted and overexploited. Irresponsible management, exacerbated by population growth, has contributed to today's health crisis: 1.3 billion people do not have access to drinking water, 2 billion not do have water treatment, and 4 billion are not connected to a treatment system. Water contaminated with malaria, diarrhea, dengue fever and other diseases is responsible for the deaths of 5 million people per year, far more than AIDS.

Improving access to water would contribute to the social development of many populations, particularly in the case of women. African women travel an average of 6 kilometres per day to provide water for their families.

This humanitarian crisis cannot be resolved through the operation of the marketplace alone. According to the World Water Forum (The Hague, 2000), 180 billion dollars per year needs to

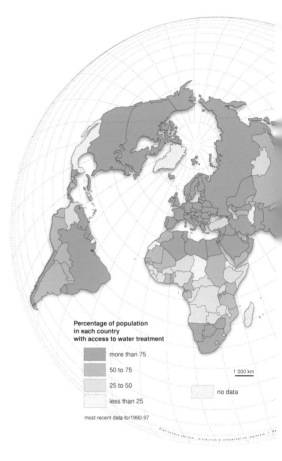

Percentage of population in each country with access to water treatment

- more than 75
- 50 to 75
- 25 to 50
- less than 25
- no data

1 000 km

most recent data for 1990-97

be invested in order to ensure full access to drinking water and conservation of resources worldwide. Only 80 billion dollars per year is currently available, and even this amount has failed to provide drinking water to the poorest countries and impoverished populations, which are unable to pay market prices.

Access to water should be given the highest priority on international political agendas. It should also be a reason for mobilisation of NGOs, communities and the local populations concerned.

Access to water is a fundamental human right. It is imperative that new public-private financial partnerships be established, taking advantage of existing structures that promote international solidarity.

Sources: PricewaterhouseCoopers, UNESCO, UNICEF, WHO

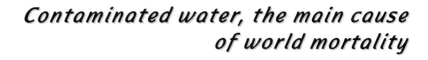

Contaminated water, the main cause of world mortality

Find out more

I in 5 people has no access to drinking water and more than I in 2 are not connected to a water treatment system.

➤ *Industrial pollution and disasters*
Ecological footprint
Water withdrawal
International solidarities

Access to drinking water

1.3 billion people do not have access to drinking water.

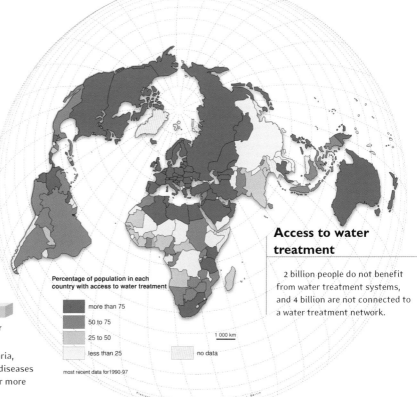

Percentage of population in each country with access to water treatment

- more than 75
- 50 to 75
- 25 to 50
- less than 25
- no data

1 000 km

most recent data for 1990-97

Access to water treatment

2 billion people do not benefit from water treatment systems, and 4 billion are not connected to a water treatment network.

Mortality due to poor water quality

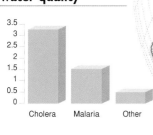

Water contaminated with malaria, cholera, dengue fever and other diseases kills 5 million people per year, far more than AIDS.

Malnutrition

815 million people were undernourished in 1999 - 17% of the world's population. In 1969, by comparison, this figure was 37%. The global improvement in agricultural productivity has reduced malnutrition figures by half. Today's average caloric intake per person is 2720 kcal. The minimum requirement, according to the FAO, is 2350 kcal.

In over 50 countries people do not manage to obtain this minimum requirement. Malnutrition has increased considerably in countries experiencing poverty and dramatic population increases. Of the 815 million people suffering from malnutrition, 777 million live in developing countries. According to UNI-CEF, 200 million of these are children.

The main reasons for malnutrition are poverty, corruption, civil wars and drought. In Sub-Saharan Africa, the results of efforts to combat malnutrition vary from success (Chad) to failure (Congo). Some countries have concentrated their resources on intensifying agricultural production, helping to create local prosperity and increasing agricultural autonomy; others have had to buy foodstuffs on the international market, while some, particularly victims of civil wars, have received foreign food aid.

Reducing inequality and poverty is the first crucial step in the fight against malnutrition. International solidarity should play a greater part in the redistribution of riches, especially through development assistance and fair trade. During the last ten years consumer associations throughout the world have initiated fair trade campaigns addressed to the general public. Through buying products (e.g. coffee, tea, chocolate) distributed according to principles of equitable commerce (pre-purchasing to safeguard networks, remuneration at a fair price, elimination of intermediaries) each consumer

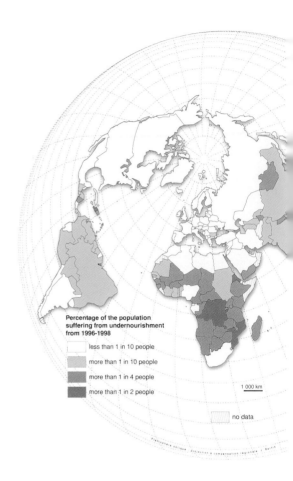

Percentage of the population suffering from undernourishment from 1996-1998

less than 1 in 10 people

more than 1 in 10 people

more than 1 in 4 people

more than 1 in 2 people

1 000 km

no data

can contribute, even if modestly, towards helping the most impoverished countries achieve agricultural autonomy.

Caloric intake levels provide a good way to judge average weight in the population of a particular country. They make it possible to identify cases of malnutrition and determine their seriousness. According to the FAO, minimum caloric supply should be 2350 kilojoules per day per person. Below this level, populations are more vulnerable to chronic disease.

Source: FAO

malnutrition

800 million people, of which 200 million are children, go hungry

Find out more

In developing countries, one out of 10 children dies before the age of five due to malnutrition.

➤ Agriculture
Inequality and poverty
International solidarities

Malnutrition

Almost one out of five people in the world suffers from malnutrition. Sub-Saharan Africa and some parts of the Asia and Pacific region have the most alarming levels of malnutrition.

Caloric intake in 1997

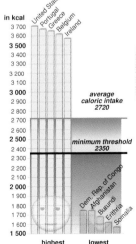

in kcal
3 700 | United States, Portugal, Greece, Belgium, Ireland
3 600
3 500
3 400
3 300
3 200
3 100
3 000 | *average caloric intake 2720*
2 900
2 800
2 700
2 600
2 500
2 400 | *minimum threshold 2350*
2 300
2 200
2 100
2 000
1 900 | Dem. Rep. of Congo, Afghanistan, Burundi, Eritria, Somalia
1 800
1 700
1 600
1 500

highest   lowest
The 10 countries in which caloric intake is:

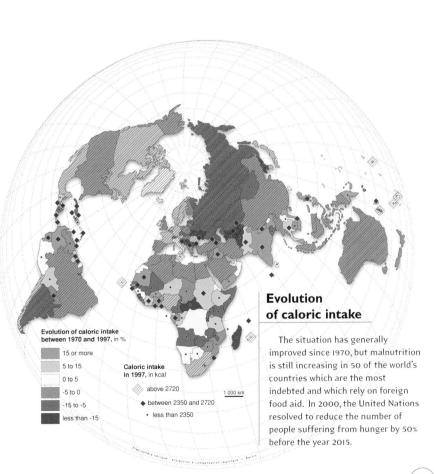

Evolution of caloric intake between 1970 and 1997, in %

- 15 or more
- 5 to 15
- 0 to 5
- -5 to 0
- -15 to -5
- less than -15

Caloric intake in 1997, in kcal

- above 2720
- ◆ between 2350 and 2720
- • less than 2350

1 000 km

Evolution of caloric intake

The situation has generally improved since 1970, but malnutrition is still increasing in 50 of the world's countries which are the most indebted and which rely on foreign food aid. In 2000, the United Nations resolved to reduce the number of people suffering from hunger by 50% before the year 2015.

17

Access to health care

Every year 17 million people die as a result of infectious diseases such as malaria, HIV/AIDS and tuberculosis. 90% of these deaths occur in developing countries, which brutally illustrates the inequalities in health access, especially access to medications.

Above all, infectious diseases essentially affect tropical and subtropical regions, which are mostly insolvent. Western pharmaceutical companies have gradually abandoned research on tropical diseases, although they are often banal and curable, due to lack of profitability.

However pharmaceutical groups continue to take a particular interest in these biodiversity-rich regions. They use these regions' plant resources and the extensive knowledge of indigenous populations to develop new molecules that will increase their profits. Several products for use in fighting cancer, for example, have been developed using Madagascan periwinkle. Price levels for pharmaceuticals, established according to the financial capacities of developed countries, are out of reach for poor countries.

The plague of infectious diseases, which has steadily worsened over the last forty years, is a challenge for public health and development policies in terms of market regulation. The United Nations and NGOs such as Médecins sans Frontières have made proposals for adapting pharmaceutical patent legislation to the situation in impoverished countries. From now on, certain African countries can produce their own patented medications without having to consider intellectual property laws.

Nevertheless most of these countries have insufficient or absolutely no capacity for detecting and treating disease. An inertia exists regarding the establishment of international financing programmes, and pharmaceutical groups resist any evolution of health market regulations: a combination which prevents any chance of impeding the African AIDS pandemic.

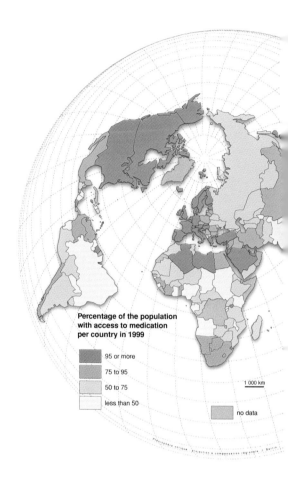

Percentage of the population with access to medication per country in 1999

- 95 or more
- 75 to 95
- 50 to 75
- less than 50
- no data

1 000 km

Public health spending

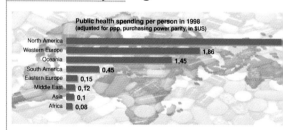

Public health spending per person in 1998
(adjusted for ppp, purchasing power parity, in $US)

North America	
Western Europe	1,86
Oceania	1,45
South America	0,45
Eastern Europe	0,15
Middle East	0,12
Asia	0,1
Africa	0,08

This study of public health expenditure does not cover the entire medical system, but figures still reveal extensive differences between continents (1 to 30).

Sources: *World Bank, Médecins sans Frontières, WHO*

For many Southern countries, medications are inaccessible

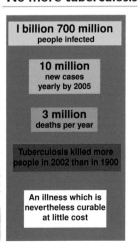

Find out more

Between 1987 and 1996, out of 1,400 newly developed medications less than 3% concerned tropical diseases.

➤ Demography
Access to water
Malnutrition
International solidarities

Access to medication

82.6% of the global pharmaceuticals market is shared by the United States (40.2%), Europe (26.6%) and Japan (15.8%). Many countries cannot afford market prices.

No more tuberculosis

I billion 700 million
people infected

10 million
new cases
yearly by 2005

3 million
deaths per year

Tuberculosis killed more people in 2002 than in 1900

An illness which is nevertheless curable at little cost

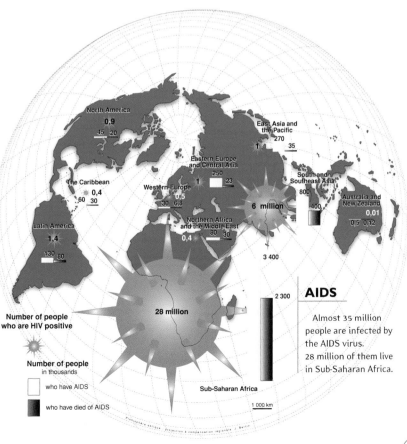

North America
0,9
45 20

East Asia and the Pacific
270
1   35

Eastern Europe and Central Asia
250
1   23

South and Southeast Asia
800

The Caribbean
0,4
60 30

Western Europe
0,5
30 6,8

Australia and New Zealand
0,01
0,5 0,12

Latin America
1,4
130 80

Northern Africa and the Middle East
0,4
80 30

6 million

400

3 400

28 million

2 300

Sub-Saharan Africa

1 000 km

Number of people who are HIV positive

Number of people
in thousands

☐ who have AIDS

■ who have died of AIDS

AIDS

Almost 35 million people are infected by the AIDS virus.
28 million of them live in Sub-Saharan Africa.

Access to education

Learning to speak and write a language is essential in order to take part in social and economic activities and act out one's role in society. In this sense, access to education is one of the most important indicators of general welfare and of sustainable development.

Figures on illiteracy and access to education reveal the enormous disparities in living standards between rich and poor countries. They also reveal serious violations of women's and children's rights. According to the International Labour Organisation and UNICEF, 250 million children in the world between 5 and 14 years old work, i.e. one in four. The proportion is highest in Africa (41%), quickly followed by Asia, which is sadly notorious for its one million children enticed into unlawful sex markets (principally in India, Thailand, Taiwan and the Philippines).

The exploitation of women and children has obviously had extensive repercussions on access to education, but it is not the only cause. If about 20% of the world's population over 15 is illiterate, and 98% of these people are in the South, nearly two thirds of this population is feminine. Children born to women who have not received any kind of schooling are twice as likely to die before their first birthday than those whose mothers have been educated beyond primary school.

While children's access to education is increasingly becoming a condition for attribution of public sector expenditure, illiteracy remains poorly funded by international aid programmes - especially as most of these programmes are aimed at the primary education sector, leaving adult literacy without resources. NGOs have had to fill the enormous gaps across the numerous regions left without any form of government assistance.

Illiteracy is also a most disturbing phenomenon

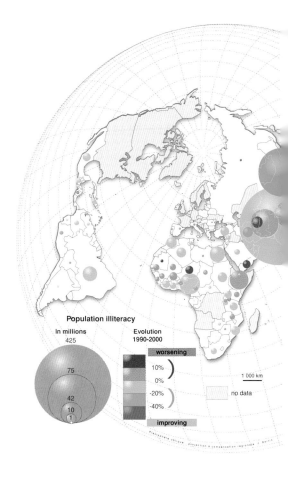

Population illiteracy

In millions
425

Evolution
1990-2000

worsening

10%
0%
-20%
-40%

1 000 km

no data

improving

in developed countries, where it is one of the aggravating factors of poverty and marginalization, leading to a divided society.

It is difficult to imagine how to achieve a better world as long as subsequent generations are not treated in a civilized way. Even more than the necessity for social or economic structures, access to education is a challenge to human dignity and the fight against exclusion, in both the North and the South.

Sources: OIT, UNESCO, UNICEF

access to education

20% of the world's population over 15 years of age is illiterate

Women's literacy

Number of literate women for every 100 men

100
97
100
73

South America   **Africa**

In Latin America, male/female equality has greatly improved in the educational domain. Africa is still a long way behind in improving its situation.

Find out more

40% of the world's children are not registered at birth.

> *Status of Women*
> *Inequality and poverty*
> *International solidarities*

Illiteracy

In developing countries access to education is still random and illiteracy levels remain high. It is useful, however, to note the net progress in India and China. Northern countries also reveal signs of illiteracy in areas of marginality and exclusion, but figures are not easily available.

*gross enrolment ratios: total enrolment at a specific level of education, regardless of age, expressed as a percentage of the official school age population corresponding to the same level of education in a given school year.

The GER can be greater than 100%, due to inclusion of over-aged and under-aged pupils/students because of early or late entrants and grade repetition. In this case, a rigorous interpretation of GER needs additional information to assess the extent of repetition, late entrants etc.

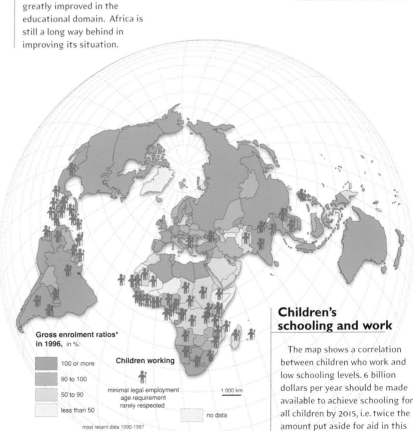

Gross enrolment ratios* in 1996, in %:

- 100 or more
- 90 to 100
- 50 to 90
- less than 50

most recent data 1990-1997

Children working

minimal legal employment age requirement rarely respected

1 000 km

no data

Children's schooling and work

The map shows a correlation between children who work and low schooling levels. 6 billion dollars per year should be made available to achieve schooling for all children by 2015, i.e. twice the amount put aside for aid in this sector by official development assistance programmes.

---

access to education

1

20% of the world's population over 15 years of age is illiterate

Women's literacy

Number of literate women for every 100 men

100
97

100
73

South America   **Africa**

In Latin America, male/female equality has greatly improved in the educational domain. Africa is still a long way behind in improving its situation.

Find out more

40% of the world's children are not registered at birth.

➤ *Status of Women*
Inequality and poverty
International solidarities

Illiteracy

In developing countries access to education is still random and illiteracy levels remain high. It is useful, however, to note the net progress in India and China. Northern countries also reveal signs of illiteracy in areas of marginality and exclusion, but figures are not easily available.

*gross enrolment ratios: total enrolment at a specific level of education, regardless of age, expressed as a percentage of the official school age population corresponding to the same level of education in a given school year.

The GER can be greater than 100%, due to inclusion of over-aged and under-aged pupils/students because of early or late entrants and grade repetition. In this case, a rigorous interpretation of GER needs additional information to assess the extent of repetition, late entrants etc.

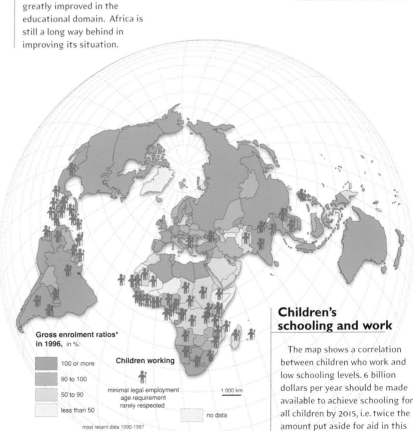

Gross enrolment ratios* in 1996, in %:

- 100 or more
- 90 to 100
- 50 to 90
- less than 50

most recent data 1990-1997

Children working

minimal legal employment age requirement rarely respected

1 000 km

no data

Children's schooling and work

The map shows a correlation between children who work and low schooling levels. 6 billion dollars per year should be made available to achieve schooling for all children by 2015, i.e. twice the amount put aside for aid in this sector by official development assistance programmes.

21

Status of women

At the conclusion of the Fourth World Conference on Women in Beijing in 1995, over 100 countries committed themselves to reinforcing women's social, economic and political power, improving their access to health and education, and promoting their civil rights. However there's still a long way to go.

Domination by men continues despite demands made by feminist groups, supported in 1979 by the United Nations convention on the elimination of all discrimination against women. Nevertheless in 2002 women do not have the right to vote in some countries.

Women control only 1% of world revenue. Even when their jobs require the same competence and responsibilities, their salaries average 25% less than men's. In view of salary differences, denial of their civil rights and lack of access to contraception or abortion, the status of women is still far from equal. On the whole, they continue to be excluded from positions of power throughout the world.

To this type of discrimination must be added male violence, of which one in five European women is a victim. Domestic violence in Europe is a more common cause of bodily harm or death among 15 to 44 year old women than cancer or automobile accidents. The Spanish social services estimate that only 10% of women overcome their fear of reprisals and report that they have been ill treated in the home. The situation is certainly worse in countries for which no data are available.

The main reasons for this type of violence, which is tolerated in many countries, are women's economic dependence, their mistreatment during childhood and men's alcoholism. Western countries have adopted measures promoting equality between boys and

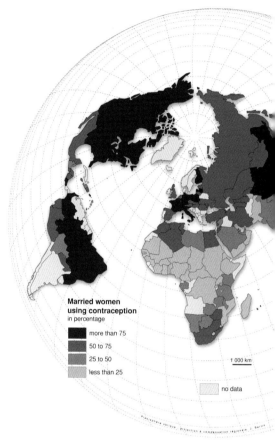

Married women using contraception
in percentage

- more than 75
- 50 to 75
- 25 to 50
- less than 25

1 000 km

- no data

girls at school and providing more security and legal aid for victims. Developing countries continue to lag far behind.

Once they have the right to speak their minds, many women become resolute defenders of peace and mutual respect.

Sexual discrimination

The Gender-related Development Index (GDI) is used with the Human Development Index (HDI). It measures and compares levels of life expectancy, literacy and education, and the level of women's incomes compared with men's. The higher the GDI, the greater the gender equality. Women in Yemen are the most discriminated against according to this index.

Sources: IPU, Population Reference Bureau, UNESCO

The majority of women are still excluded from knowledge and power

Find out more

Of the 185 high-ranking diplomats at the United Nations, seven are women.

➤ *Access to education*
Social malaise
Conflict

Use of contraception

In Africa, use of contraception is below 20% in every Sub-Saharan country. In the same countries one in 16 women dies due to problems during pregnancy or delivery, compared to one in 1,400 in Europe.

nine countries where sexual discrimination is most extreme

difference between the Gender-related Development Index (GDI) and the Human Development Index (HDI)

Yemen	**-58**
Saudi Arabia	**-35**
Oman	**-32**
Guinea-Bissau	**-31**
Sudan	**-29**
Syria	**-23**
Libya	**-22**
Belize	**-21**
Algeria	**-20**

Discrimination is considered extreme when the GDI is inferior to the HDI and the difference is greater than 20 points.

Period in which women obtained the right to vote

- after 1970
- between 1950 and 1970
- between 1930 and 1950
- before 1930
- women's right to vote not recognized

1 000 km

no data

The Right to Vote

In 1893, New Zealand was the first country to give women the right to vote. Women finally obtained the right to vote in Qatar on 8 March 1999.

Freedom of the press

Freedom of expression and freedom of the press indicate the degree of democracy existing within political regimes. How can people fulfil their responsibilities as citizens and fully participate in public life without access to information or the right to free speech? Countries that want to be United Nations members must now include freedom of expression in their constitution or legislation. Many regimes, however, have discovered ideological or judicial reasons to reduce such commitments.

Russia, for example, has reassured the press countless times that it will respect its independence, while explaining that "information must serve the national interest". Cuban law guarantees freedom of expression and information, but insists they "should be used in accordance with the objectives of a socialist society". In the view of Chinese leaders, the role of journalists is to "serve the people". In Nigeria, where the charia has the force of law, journalists "causing harm to Islamic values" may be punished by being beaten.

Macedonia has introduced a misdemeanour offense for lack of professionalism, while in Latin America "the honour of civil servants" is protected by laws whose legitimacy has been brought into question during blackmail or money laundering affairs. Myanmar (Burma) has a law under which imprisonment can be incurred for supplying "incorrect information".

The most recent annual report from Reporters Without Borders (Reporters sans Frontières - RSF), which covers 189 countries, describes an alarming situation in which those in power (heads of state, military leaders, armed groups) take repressive actions against the press. Internet, the perfect medium for the struggle against censorship, has become the object of a whole array of repressive responses in some countries. North Korea must be the gold medallist in this regard, as Internet access is simply banned in that country. Saudi Arabia has chosen to construct a gigantic system to filter addresses and content. China has even introduced the death penalty for "cybercriminals".

518 journalists killed in 10 years

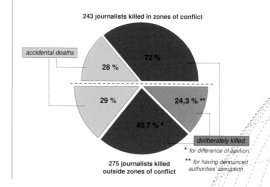

243 journalists killed in zones of conflict

accidental deaths

72 %

28 %

29 %

24,3 % **

46,7 % *

deliberately killed
* for difference of opinion
** for having denounced authorities' corruption

275 journalists killed outside zones of conflict

journalists killed, which media?

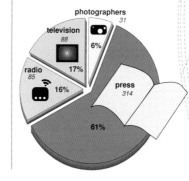

photographers
31

television
88

6%

radio
85

17%

16%

press
314

61%

Find out more

In March 2002, 96 journalists and 24 "cyberdissidents" (journalists, cyber cafe operators, net surfers) were imprisoned for their opinions in Burma, China, Iran and Nepal.

➤ *Conflict*
   Corruption

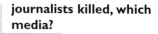

One third of the global population lives in countries where freedom of the press is repressed

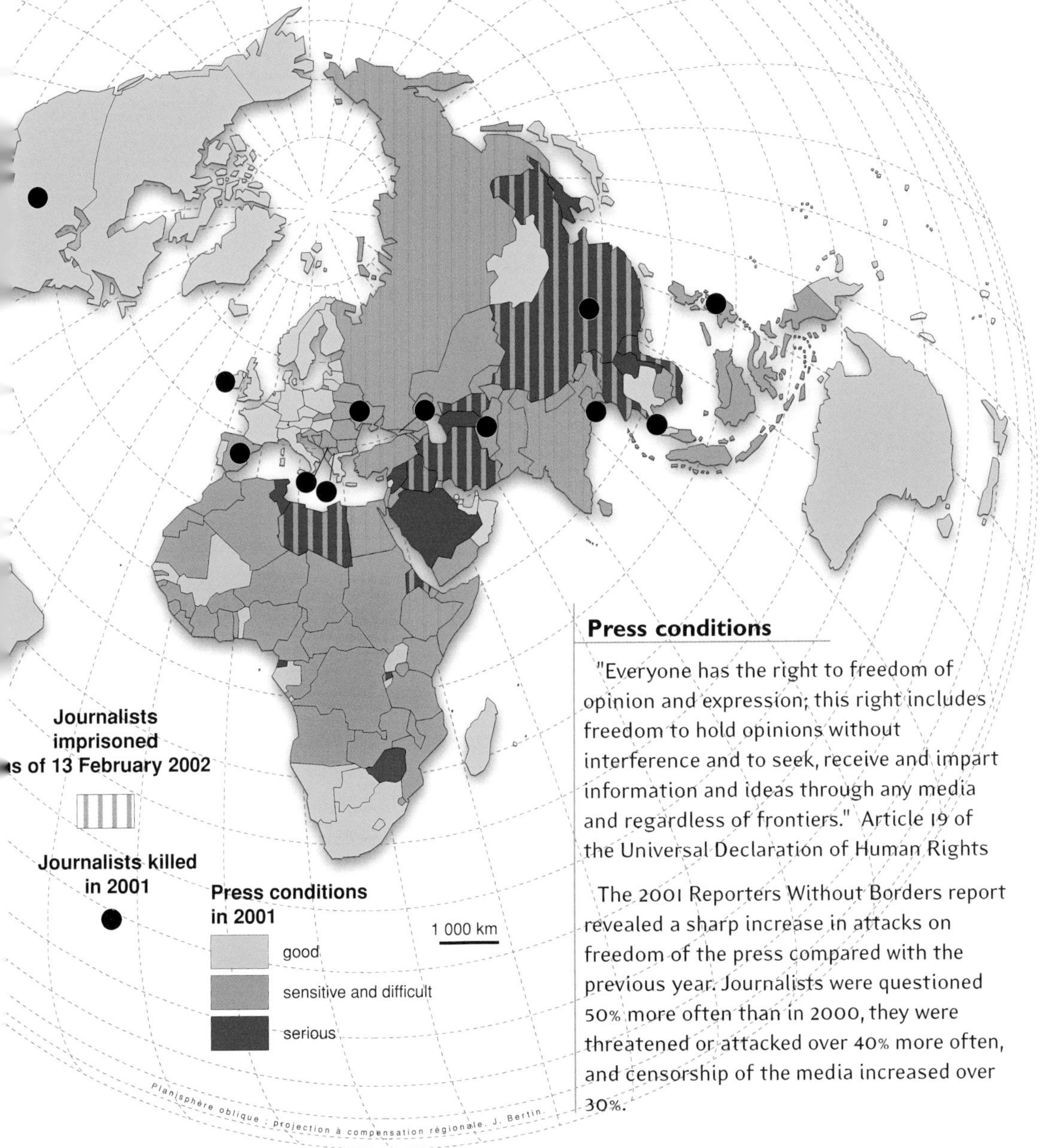

Journalists
imprisoned
as of 13 February 2002

Journalists killed
in 2001

Press conditions
in 2001

1 000 km

good

sensitive and difficult

serious

Planisphère oblique ; projection à compensation régionale ; J. Bertin

Press conditions

"Everyone has the right to freedom of opinion and expression; this right includes freedom to hold opinions without interference and to seek, receive and impart information and ideas through any media and regardless of frontiers." Article 19 of the Universal Declaration of Human Rights

The 2001 Reporters Without Borders report revealed a sharp increase in attacks on freedom of the press compared with the previous year. Journalists were questioned 50% more often than in 2000, they were threatened or attacked over 40% more often, and censorship of the media increased over 30%.

Source: Reporters Without Borders

25

Social malaise

Violence (both psychological and physical) affects every region in the world. It leads to attacks on human dignity and to social malaise in the form of poverty, exclusion, psychological collapse, drug and alcohol abuse, and the effects on those exposed to armed conflict and racial or sexual discrimination. In 1999 there were 1.7 million suicides and homicide victims, most of them young men.

Homicides occur mainly in major urban areas, especially in countries where possession of firearms is allowed. Homicide rates in Japan, the United States and Brazil are 0.6, 7 and 25 per 100,000 inhabitants, respectively.

Women and children are also subjected to violence: it is estimated that 40 million children per year are victims of aggression and sexual abuse, while roughly one third of the world's women are targets of violence at some time in their lives. While these figures can serve as estimates, many aggressive acts are neither reported nor discouraged, especially in cases of abuse within families, including in western countries.

2001 saw its share of violence within the frame-work of armed conflicts: the second Intifada in the Middle East, civil wars in Burundi and Guinea, open conflict in Congo, and rene-wed fighting in Chechnya. Torture was repor-ted in over 150 countries, and journalists were imprisoned or murdered.

General mobilization of the international community is needed in favour of the struggle against violence, including calls for limitations on arms expenditure and on use of firearms, together with a campaign against urban exclu-sion and renewed support for access to edu-cation.

Find out more

In São Paolo homicides are the primary cause of death amongst young men 16 to 24 years of age.

➤ *Status of women*
Freedom of the press
Conflict

Suicide rates are three times higher amongst men than women

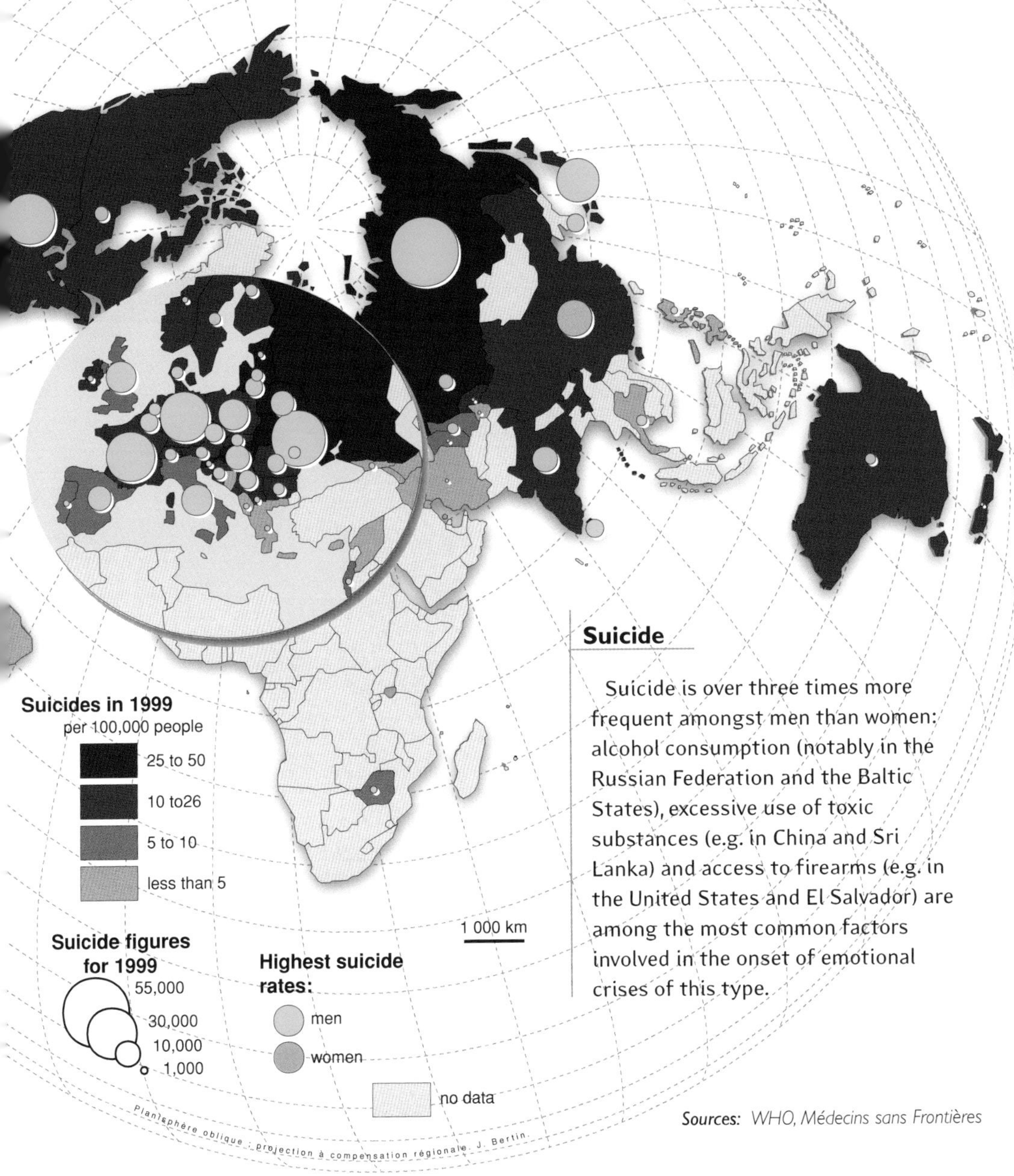

Suicides in 1999
per 100,000 people

- 25 to 50
- 10 to26
- 5 to 10
- less than 5

Suicide figures for 1999

- 55,000
- 30,000
- 10,000
- 1,000

1 000 km

Highest suicide rates:

- men
- women

no data

Plansphère oblique - projection à compensation régionale J. Bertin

Suicide

Suicide is over three times more frequent amongst men than women: alcohol consumption (notably in the Russian Federation and the Baltic States), excessive use of toxic substances (e.g. in China and Sri Lanka) and access to firearms (e.g. in the United States and El Salvador) are among the most common factors involved in the onset of emotional crises of this type.

Sources: WHO, *Médecins sans Frontières*

27

WORLD ATLAS OF SUSTAINABLE DEVELOPMENT

Conflict

One of the principles upheld at the "Earth Summit" in Rio was that peace, sustainable development and environmental protection are interdependent and cannot be disassociated.

The press rarely fails to report on wide-scale loss of human life, while conflicts' environmental and economic impact is seldom mentioned and information is often concealed for reasons of state security. For example, air force maneuvers are not subject to control and evaluation of their impact on global warming, air pollution and noise pollution. The military sector is the main producer of chemical and nuclear waste. Training and military exercises represent 10% of total fossil fuel consumption.

The world has a responsibility to future generations, but the devastating impacts of war go against such principles. The herbicide "Agent Orange", widely used to destroy vegetation during the Vietnam War, still has a deteriorating effect thirty years on. Bombs, chemical weapons and antipersonnel mines kill and mutilate civilians, pollute the soil, and therefore deprive populations of their earning capacities.

Economically, arms expenditure absorbs large portions of governmental budgets to the detriment of vital investment in health, education and the environment. Morocco dedicates 4.8% of its GDP to arms expenditure, Iran 5.23%. While poverty and inequality continue to increase in the North as well as the South, the arms trade is flourishing. In 2000 arms budgets totalled 750 million dollars. Although 1.2 billion people worldwide live on less than one dollar per day, the United States spends three dollars per day per inhabitant on defence.

Wars, ethnic conflict and terrorism are part of a huge industry entailing the destruction of human, economic and environmental resources. Promotion of sustainable development should imply a commitment to restore peace and disarmament.

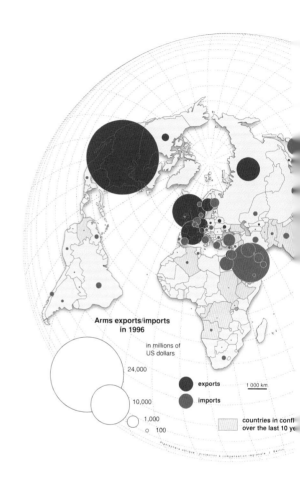

Arms exports/imports in 1996

in millions of US dollars

24,000

10,000

1,000

100

● exports
● imports

1 000 km

countries in confl[ict] over the last 10 ye[ars]

Find out more

The 1994 Rwandan wars left over one million dead.

Today's conflicts have led to the displacement of over 50 million refugees.

➤ *Social Malaise*
A question of priority: education, health or defence

War has intrinsically destructive effects on sustainable development

Number of deaths

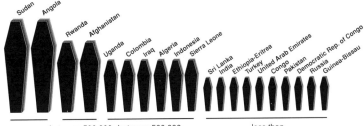

Sudan Angola Rwanda Afghanistan Uganda Colombia Iraq Algeria Indonesia Sierra Leone Sri Lanka India Ethiopia-Eritrea Turkey United Arab Emirates Congo Pakistan Democratic Rep. of Congo Russia Guinea-Bissau

over 1 million	between 500,000 and 1 million	between 500,000 and 100,000	less than 100,000

Wars in the Gulf, the Near-East, Angola, Rwanda, Congo, Kosovo and Chechenya are examples of conflicts which continue to break out over the years...

The arms market

The countries which sell the most arms are the United States (37.2%, 31.5 billion dollars), Russia (19.8%, 16.8 billion dollars) and France (11.5%, 9.7 billion dollars).

Nearly two thirds of these arms are bought by developing countries. Those which have purchased the most arms are the United Arab Emirates, India and Egypt.

Ottawa Convention on 10th October 2001

ratified

not ratified

Mines present

1 000 km

zones most affected

zones where the problem is serious

zones where the problem is less serious

Mines

The Ottawa Convention was adopted in 1997 and came into effect in 1999. It forbids signatory governments from using, stocking, producing or transferring antipersonnel mines. Countries still stocking such mines are required to destroy them within the next four years (before the end of 2003). By 2001, 141 governments had signed the Convention and 117 had ratified it. Russia, the United States, India and China chose not to participate.

Sources : IISS, IRIS, SIPRI

Through ignorance, irresponsibility and cynicism, human beings and the industries they have developed have overexploited the planet's resources to the point of exhaustion. Consequently our environment is degraded, risks have increased, and the lives of future generations have been compromised. We could arrive at a point of no return. It is clear that existing modes of production and consumption must be changed. Sustainable development is a call to order: we live in a finite, fragile and precious world.
Our survival depends on it.

Risk and the Environment

Natural disasters

Between 1991 and 2000 nearly 700,000 people, 83% of them in Asia, were killed as a result of natural disasters, including floods, landslides, volcanic eruptions, storms, cyclones, earthquakes and fires.

These catastrophes have always occurred, but the scientific community has concluded that their scale has now increased considerably. Climate change is considered to contribute to the violence of storms, cyclones and other such weather events. Development policies should also be held partly responsible: flood damage, for example, is worst in regions where there has been deforestation (one function of forests is to retain rainwater), and in urban areas where the soil has become impermeable and can no longer act as a "natural sponge" when humid zones dry out.

The rural exodus and the density of urban populations have contributed to the increase in the number of victims. According to the United Nations Environment Programme, between 30% and 60% of the inhabitants of the great Southern megalopolises live in accommodations which have been constructed without permits, including in zones subject to earthquakes or flooding. Whatever the causes of natural upheavals, it is the poorest countries which pay the highest price in loss of human life and the developed countries which pay the greatest financial costs. 67% of deaths related to natural disasters occur in developing countries.

The environmental impact of human activities must be better understood and controlled: the anarchic development of cities, limitless growth of the transport sector, and deforestation have led to a malfunctioning of nature, which has begun to turn against man.

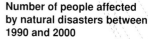

Find out more

Armed conflicts kill three times as many people as natural disasters.

▶ *Conflict*
Forests
Climate change
Urban environment
Transport

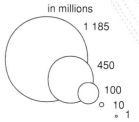

Number of people affected by natural disasters between 1990 and 2000

in millions

1 185

450

100

10

1

Sources: UNEP, Red Cross

In the 1990s the cost of natural disasters increased tenfold

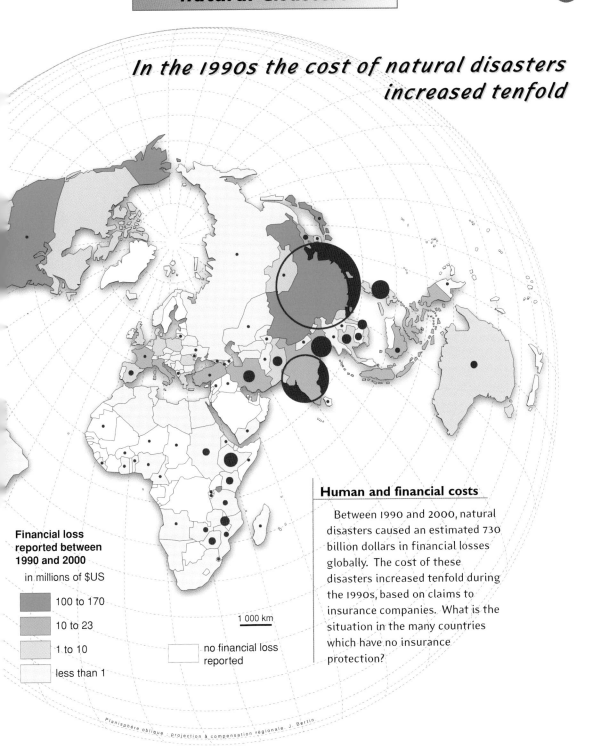

Human and financial costs

Between 1990 and 2000, natural disasters caused an estimated 730 billion dollars in financial losses globally. The cost of these disasters increased tenfold during the 1990s, based on claims to insurance companies. What is the situation in the many countries which have no insurance protection?

Financial loss reported between 1990 and 2000

in millions of $US

- 100 to 170
- 10 to 23
- 1 to 10
- less than 1

no financial loss reported

1 000 km

Planisphère oblique - Projection à compensation régionale. J. Bertin

Industrial pollution and disasters

Toxic gas emissions and explosions, oil spills and diffuse pollution... it appears that the lessons of the past have not been enough to bring about the elimination of industrial pollution and disasters

On 3 December 1984 thousands of people were killed and hundreds of thousands were exposed to health risks when a toxic chemical was accidentally released at the Union Carbide pesticide plant in Bhopal, India. On 26 April 1986, in Chernobyl (Ukraine), the worst nuclear disaster in history occurred, followed by an unprecedented campaign of disinformation in the former USSR as well as in Europe. In 1991, during the Gulf War, Iraq deliberately released 800,000 tonnes of oil off the coast of Kuwait (by comparison, 230,000 tonnes was spilled off the French coast in 1978 when the Amoco Cadiz ran aground).

Generally speaking, diffuse pollution resulting from industrial activities has far more severe impacts than do industrial accidents. Industrial production of toxic substances (e.g. CO_2, herbicides and pesticides) is the origin of the diffuse pollution that contaminates water, air and soil and threatens health via inhalation or food contamination. An international convention banning a dozen toxic substances known as POPs (persistent organic pollutants) was recently agreed.

Increasing levels of risk have brought about an overall loss of confidence in the industrial sector. Negotiations for victims' compensation entail a bargaining process, during which whole populations remain in distress. The safety of installations, corporate responsibility, and the effectiveness of national and international regulations are increasingly being called into question. Civil society is demanding better risk prevention measures and protection of affected populations.

Principal technological disasters during the last 10 years

    oil spills

    industrial accidents

    nuclear accidents

1 000 km

Are we condemned to live with these risks? Zero risk does not exist, but those in charge can no longer continue to avoid their responsibilities. Environmental and consumer NGOs are expanding their boycott campaigns, and there is growing pressure from within the financial sector. Several large groups have begun to put risk prevention initiatives in place, coordinating their efforts with employees and neighbouring populations.

Sources: CRED, Red Cross, ITOPF, OECD

Degassing tanks at sea produces ten times as much pollution as oil spills

Find out more

Chemical pollution does not respect frontiers: traces of DDT (a highly powerful toxic insecticide) have been identified in the fatty tissue of Antarctic penguins

> Seas and oceans
> Waste
> Energy production and consumption

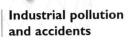

Industrial pollution and accidents

The coasts of the Atlantic and the North Sea have been the most affected by oil spills. European NGOs are demanding that the responsibility of tanker operators be made clearer.

Emissions of sulphur compounds

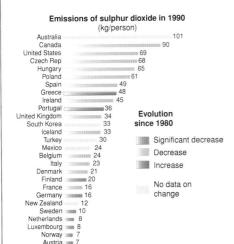

Emissions of sulphur dioxide in 1990 (kg/person)

Australia	101
Canada	90
United States	69
Czech Rep	68
Hungary	65
Poland	61
Spain	49
Greece	48
Ireland	45
Portugal	36
United Kingdom	34
South Korea	33
Iceland	33
Turkey	30
Mexico	24
Belgium	24
Italy	23
Denmark	21
Finland	20
France	16
Germany	16
New Zealand	12
Sweden	10
Netherlands	8
Luxembourg	8
Norway	7
Austria	7
Switzerland	5

Evolution since 1980

- Significant decrease
- Decrease
- Increase
- No data on change

Emissions of sulphur compounds produce acid rain and affect air and water quality, as well as posing serious health risks. Some progress has been made: diffuse pollution has been reduced considerably over the last 20 years.

CFCs

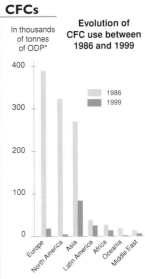

In thousands of tonnes of ODP*

Evolution of CFC use between 1986 and 1999

- 1986
- 1999

ODP: Ozone depletion potential

Sometimes perseverance pays off. In the 1970s researchers revealed the toxicity of CFCs (chlorofluorocarbons), manufactured for use as coolants, solvents and aerosol propellants. CFCs destroy the ozone layer that protects us from solar ultraviolet radiation. The 1987 Montreal Protocol has led to the elimination of these chemicals in developed countries (they are to be phased out in developing countries by 2010).

Seas and Oceans

Seas and oceans, rivers and lakes, ponds, marshes and wetlands are all essential for our planet to function. The Ramsar Convention on Wetlands of International Importance, adopted in 1971, has been ratified by 131 countries

A large part of our food supply comes from the sea. The availability of these resources depends on the quality of marine ecosystems, which are threatened above all by hydrocarbon pollution, construction in coastal areas and over-fishing.

Ships emptying their tanks illegally at sea are responsible for creating ten times as much pollution as that represented by oil slicks. Six million tonnes of hydrocarbons are dumped into the oceans every year. Some 1,000 ships empty their tanks in the Mediterranean annually. Inadequate surveillance ensures that few offenders are convicted. The tourist industry has an insatiable appetite for space.

Camping sites, hotels and car parks threaten coastal ecosystems. Having built up its coastal areas for decades, France (the world's most popular tourist destination) created a Coastal Conservatory in 1976. This State institution purchases coastal zones to preserve them from urban pressure.

The fishing industry, like many others, must meet the challenge of sustainable development: how to ensure a decent living for fishermen at the same time as healthy food products and the survival of marine species? According to the European Commission, the European fleet should be reduced by 40% to permit the renewal of fishery resources. One of the perverse effects of overexploitation is that European boats, with their superior fishing techniques, are now working along the African coast where they threaten local fishing.

Finally, coral reefs, which are indispensable for economic stability in many regions of the world,

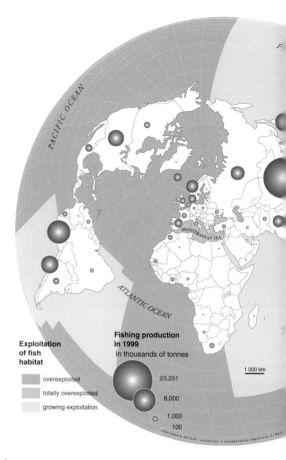

are highly fragile ecosystems endangered by climate change.

The El Niño events, by increasing the temperature of Pacific waters, have severely damaged the reefs, especially those off the coast of Australia.

Find out more

Overfishing has forced Canada to ban cod catches off the coast of Newfoundland

▶ *Industrial pollution and disasters*
Climate change

Sources: *Australian Institute of Marine Science, European Commission, FAO, UNEP, WWRI*

Overfishing today threatens the future of fishing

Fish stocks
(depletion of stocks in %, in 1999)

in percentage
total = 100%

recovering stock	1
depleted stock	9
overfishing	18
full capacity fishing	47
moderate fishing	21
underexploited	4

Of the nearly 600 fish stocks monitored by the FAO in different zones, 74% (47%, 18% and 9%) of catches are considered to be overexploited.

Overfishing

A large number of fish stocks have been exhausted or severely damaged. Before the 1950s the problem was confined to certain regions. Today fishermen catch six times as much as they did half a century ago. The fishing industry has developed quickly, and fish stocks are decreasing throughout the world.

Mangroves

Mangrove swamps are found along 8% of the world's coastlines and a quarter of tropical coastlines. These forest ecosystems are of crucial importance for tropical fishing and coastal stabilization. As a result of human pressures they have been reduced considerably. Half the world's mangroves have disappeared

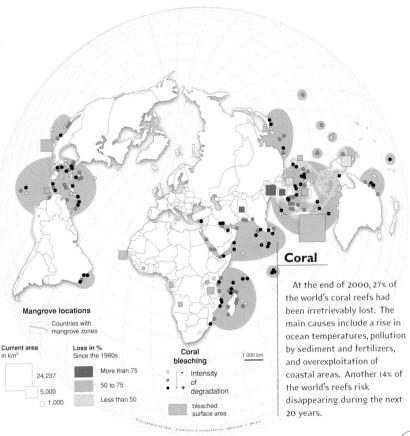

Mangrove locations

Countries with mangrove zones

Current area
in km²

24,237

5,000

1,000

Loss in %
Since the 1980s

More than 75

50 to 75

Less than 50

Coral bleaching

○ | - Intensity
● | + of degradation

1 000 km

bleached surface area

Planisphère oblique : projection à compensation regionale / Berlin

Coral

At the end of 2000, 27% of the world's coral reefs had been irretrievably lost. The main causes include a rise in ocean temperatures, pollution by sediment and fertilizers, and overexploitation of coastal areas. Another 14% of the world's reefs risk disappearing during the next 20 years.

Desertification

Desertification is spreading across 70% of the world's arid land (some 3,600 million hectares). While every continent experiences desertification, Africa is the most vulnerable. Over 800 million people are affected by this phenomenon, which, whatever its causes, invariably leads to loss of arable land, loss of fertility and extended poverty.

Desertification is the result of both climatic and human factors. Although it mainly affects arid zones, it can also occur in humid regions. Villagers in some tropical regions clear the land of trees to enlarge their fields, as agriculture is their only source of revenue. As the years pass, the soil is impoverished and a vicious circle begins: agricultural yield diminishes, leading to yet more clearing and loss of vegetation, and desertification continues to increase.

Another cause of desertification is explosive population growth in arid regions, which leads to overgrazing. Livestock breeding requires an increasing number of waterholes, eventually causing the soil to dry up. Populations lose their means of production and nourishment and move on to already overpopulated urban areas.

Village communities and farmers need to be fully involved in combating desertification. Organizations such as the Global Environment Facility finance livestock breeding and sustainable farming programmes aimed at resource renewal. At the Rio Earth Summit in 1992 those countries most affected by the problem proposed a convention to address vegetation decline and soil infertility. This convention, adopted in Paris in 1994, was signed by 170 countries.

There are strong connections between desertification, deforestation, loss of the planet's biodiversity and climate change. There are international conventions to deal with each of these issues. Numerous actors are demanding more effective synergies between such crucial problems and the conventions created to resolve them.

Find out more

In 1994 an international network of NGOs was created in Ouagadougou (Burkina Faso) to fight desertification (INBO).

➤ Forests
  Climate change
  Inequality and poverty

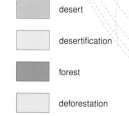

Degradation of natural habitat

▢	desert
▢	desertification
▣	forest
▢	deforestation

Sources: UN, INBO

One third of the world's visible land is affected by desertification

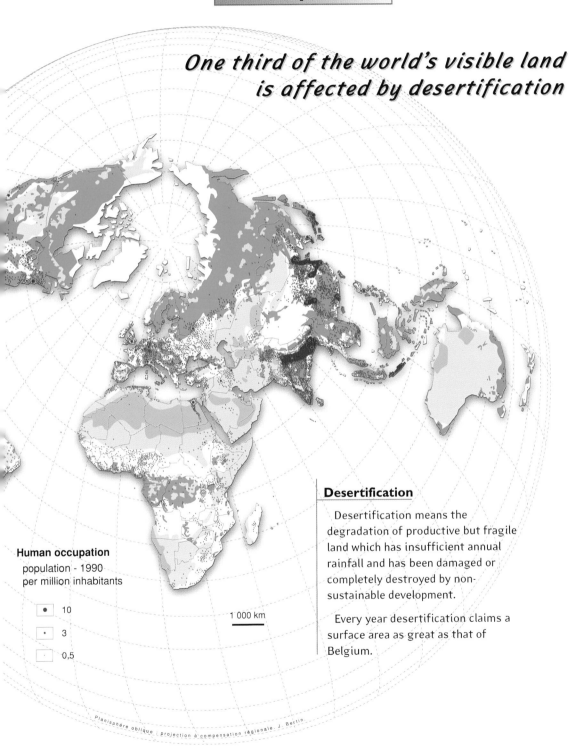

Human occupation

population - 1990
per million inhabitants

- 10
- 3
- 0,5

1 000 km

Planisphère oblique : projection à compensation régionale, J. Bertin

Desertification

Desertification means the degradation of productive but fragile land which has insufficient annual rainfall and has been damaged or completely destroyed by non-sustainable development.

Every year desertification claims a surface area as great as that of Belgium.

Forests

Forests cover 30% of the planet's terrestrial surface - 3,870 million hectares. They play an essential role, protecting a large part of the world's biological diversity and helping absorb CO_2 emissions.

Since the 1990s an estimated 9.4 million hectares per year of forested area has been lost, a problem of increasing concern to climatologists, biologists and environmental NGOs.

In 1998, El Niño resulted in an intense drought and catastrophic fires entailing human, ecological and economic loss: Latin America and Southeast Asia were badly affected. Violent storms in 1999 uprooted thousands of trees across Europe. In 2000, 200 million hectares of forest in southern Africa were destroyed by fire.

Of course human activity is greatly to blame: for thousands of years forests have been felled for agriculture and to obtain wood and firewood - the only energy source available in many countries. In temperate countries deforestation decreased in the 20th century due to growing diversification of the raw materials needed for fuel or construction. There has even been an increase in forested areas (new plantations), although this has often been detrimental to the variety of species.

Deforestation in tropical and subtropical forests is primarily due to overexploitation of forests to obtain tropical wood, which is of the greatest commercial interest, and illegal cutting. The most impoverished rural populations will clear even the most unproductive land to survive.

Several NGOs and countries have introduced a labelling system that certifies origin, in order to ensure sustainable forest management. Although implemented on a relatively small scale so far - just 2% of forests are protected by such labels - this is a sign of increased awareness. At the same time, forest management pro-

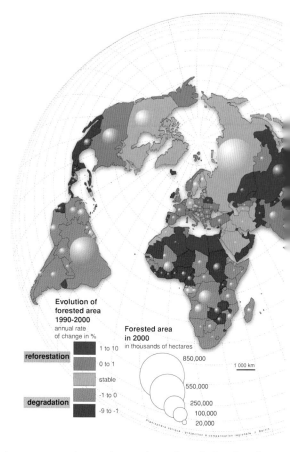

Evolution of forested area 1990-2000
annual rate of change in %

reforestation
- 1 to 10
- 0 to 1
- stable

degradation
- -1 to 0
- -9 to -1

Forested area in 2000
in thousands of hectares
- 850,000
- 550,000
- 250,000
- 100,000
- 20,000

1 000 km

grammes have been introduced in Brazil, Mongolia and Namibia to encourage villagers to learn the best clearing practices while reinforcing fire prevention. Finally, international trade in wood should be subject to a stricter regulatory framework.

Global forest distribution

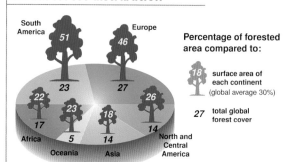

South America 51
Europe 46
23 27
22 26
17 23 18 14
Africa 5 14 North and Central America
Oceania Asia

Percentage of forested area compared to:

18 surface area of each continent (global average 30%)

27 total global forest cover

Today only 2% of the world's forests are certified

Find out more

Congo, in order to repay its international debt, overexploits its forests to such an extent that they may completely disappear by 2050.

➤ Biodiversity
Climate change
Dependency

Evolution of forested area

Every year about 10 million hectares of forest cover disappears. Tropical forests are being destroyed at a rate of nearly 1% per year.

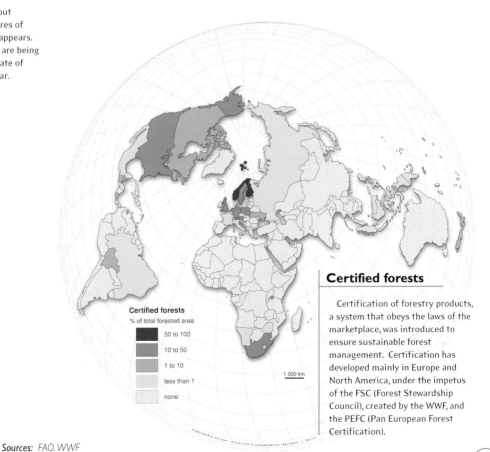

Certified forests
% of total forested area

- 50 to 100
- 10 to 50
- 1 to 10
- less than 1
- none

1 000 km

Certified forests

Certification of forestry products, a system that obeys the laws of the marketplace, was introduced to ensure sustainable forest management. Certification has developed mainly in Europe and North America, under the impetus of the FSC (Forest Stewardship Council), created by the WWF, and the PEFC (Pan European Forest Certification).

Sources: FAO, WWF

Biodiversity

"Action has to be taken without delay and with determination to preserve genes, species and ecosystems for the future management and sustainable employment of biological resources" (Chapter XV of Agenda 21, adopted at Rio).

Nature is a precious reservoir, on which numerous species depend for food and medication. 75% of edible plants comes from just seven plants (wheat, corn, potatoes, barley, sweet potatoes, manioc); western medicine extracts 50% of its products from 119 active constituents in plants, or from the synthesis of such substances.

Of the 1.7 billion known species, over 11,000 animal and plant species are threatened with extinction in the short term (only 10% of animal and plant species have thus far been identified). According to the World Conservation Union, two to three species become extinct every hour. If this trend continues, half the Earth's species will become extinct during the 21st century.

The main cause of biodiversity loss is the degradation or disappearance of natural habitats as a result of deforestation, intensive agriculture and fishing, mining extraction, drainage of humid zones, etc. Animal trafficking (e.g. monkeys, birds, reptiles, turtles) has aggravated the problem, although international conventions on the protection of threatened species have begun to have an effect.

The disappearance of natural habitats is mainly due to the transformation of forests into pastures or arable land, which jeopardizes the survival of 83% of mammals and 85% of rare birds. Humid zones are natural habitats that provide shelter to a great variety of different species. Alarmed by the state of such areas, which are increasingly threatened and fragile, the international community agreed in the Ramsar Convention to protect wetlands of importance.

Percentage of land protected

- 20 or more
- 10 to 20
- 5 to 10
- less than 5
- no data

1 000 km

Natural areas are also the home of numerous populations (e.g. minority ethnic groups in South America and Africa) which, if their habitats became degraded, would be condemned to disappear - and, along with them, their culture, knowledge and way of life.

The United Nations Environment Programme (UNEP) report on The Future of the Global Environment presents some troubling conclusions: "Many of the planet's species have already become extinct or are threatened with extinction, due to the amount of time it takes for the environment to reconstruct itself, or for decisions to be taken; it is already too late to preserve all aspects of the planet's rich biological diversity."

Over 11,000 species of plants and animals are threatened with extinction in the short term

Find out more

The elephant population of Africa in 1970 was 2.5 million, but by 1995 it was only 580,000. Since then, a ban on trade in ivory has prevented extinction

▶ *Health care*
Forests
Ecological footprint
Agriculture

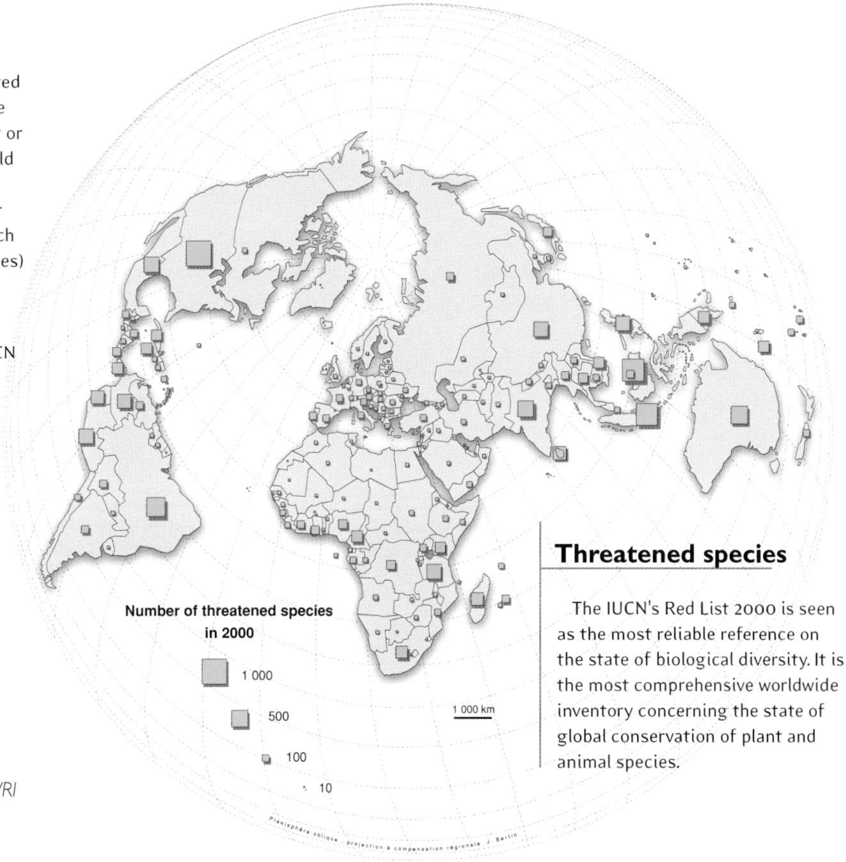

Protected areas

The World Conservation Union (IUCN) defines "protected areas" as land or sea zones which are especially dedicated to the protection and conservation of biological diversity and associated cultural resources, and which are organized according to efficient or legal measures. These areas could be national parks, natural or cultural monuments, and land or marine landscapes, some of which (like UNESCO's biosphere reserves) are also protected by global treaties,

It should be noted that the IUCN inventory lists areas for which levels of protection differ enormously.

Number of threatened species in 2000

1 000

500

1 000 km

100

10

Threatened species

The IUCN's Red List 2000 is seen as the most reliable reference on the state of biological diversity. It is the most comprehensive worldwide inventory concerning the state of global conservation of plant and animal species.

Sources: IUCN, UNEP, UNO, WRI

Climate change

Scientists estimate that we emit 28 billion tonnes of greenhouse gases (CO_2, methane, CFCs, nitrogen oxides) to the atmosphere to meet our transport, heating, air conditioning, agricultural and industrial needs.

These emissions – there is now unanimous agreement within the scientific community – contribute to global warming. During the 21st century it is estimated that the global surface temperature could increase by 2 to 6°C. The consequences of global warming will affect a vast majority of the planet's population, particularly those living in island states or littoral zones threatened with immersion and therefore with disappearing. Two thirds of the Pacific islands will face such a situation.

In 1997, within the framework of the Climate Change Convention adopted at Rio, the Kyoto Protocol committed industrialized countries to reduce their greenhouse gas emissions by 2010. Several governments and lobbies are opposed to this commitment, owing to the requirements for significant investment in clean technology and controls on heavy industry.

This subject has suddenly become especially newsworthy due to the repeated extreme climatic phenomena experienced since 1998: e.g. flooding in China and the Middle East, fires in Indonesia, Brazil and Australia, cyclones in Central America, droughts in Mongolia and Texas, storms in Europe. The world is discovering that nature reacts excessively to human excess.

In 2001 in Marrakech, and despite the refusal of the United States (which produces over one third of global greenhouse gas emissions) to take part, a protocol was adopted and implemented. As an economic instrument administering risk and pollution control, it could foreshadow an eventual global organization with respect to the environment which would take into consideration - beyond national or private sector interests - the interests of future generations and the preservation of life on Earth.

CO_2 emissions from transport

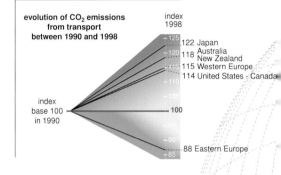

evolution of CO_2 emissions from transport between 1990 and 1998

index 1998

index base 100 in 1990

- 125
- 122 Japan
- 120 118 Australia
- New Zealand
- 115 Western Europe
- 114 United States - Canada
- 110
- 105
- 100
- 90
- 88 Eastern Europe
- 85

Find out more

Two thirds of Pacific islands are at risk of immersion due to global warming

▶ *Forests*
Waste
Ecological footprint
Energy production and consumption
Agriculture
Transport

The temperature could increase by 2 to 6°C during the 21st century

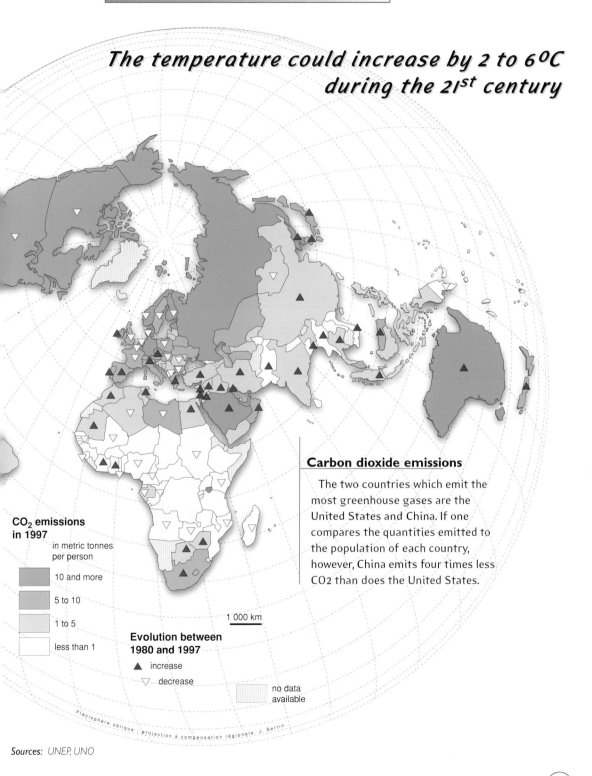

Carbon dioxide emissions

The two countries which emit the most greenhouse gases are the United States and China. If one compares the quantities emitted to the population of each country, however, China emits four times less CO2 than does the United States.

CO₂ emissions in 1997

in metric tonnes per person

- 10 and more
- 5 to 10
- 1 to 5
- less than 1

1 000 km

Evolution between 1980 and 1997

▲ increase

▽ decrease

no data available

Planisphère oblique : projection à compensation régionale. J. Bertin

Sources: UNEP, UNO

45

Waste

Growth in consumerism, coupled with intensive industrialization and urbanization, have systematically led to excessive domestic waste production.

In cities and countries where waste treatment is inadequate or insufficient, a number of harmful effects can result: water, air and soil pollution, hygiene and health risks, noxious odours, and degradation of the natural and urban environment. Rubbish dumps produce emissions of methane (a greenhouse gas) and can contaminate soil and ground water. Incineration, too, damages the environment. Industrial and hospital waste is especially toxic.

Some progress has been made with respect to waste management through public information campaigns, selective sorting, recycling, and the use of fuel substitutes. But these results have little significance compared with the tonnage being produced. Sustainable management of waste will require drastic reduction of waste production and the development of "clean" products: that is, products that are completely recyclable or need very little packaging.

Some industrial sectors, such as construction and automobile production, have begun to implement regulations or use labelling to facilitate waste recycling. The nuclear industry has not yet determined how to treat its waste.

Waste treatment is a major issue for manufacturers and for industrialized countries. Costs are very high, people do not want waste treatment plants on their doorsteps, and regulations are increasingly strict. There was extensive illegal trafficking of hazardous waste in the 1980s, with toxic waste being sent to the South from industrialized countries. Signatories of the Basel Convention (which came into effect in 1992) have agreed to restrict both production and transport of toxic waste.

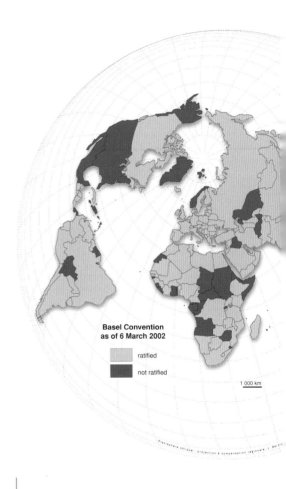

Basel Convention as of 6 March 2002

▢ ratified

◼ not ratified

1 000 km

Methane

Evolution of anthropogenic methane emissions between 1990 and 1998, in %

+3,6	-0,9	-10	-15,5	-30,8
United States Canada	Australia New Zealand	Japan	Western Europe	Eastern Europe

By volume, methane is the third most important contributor to the greenhouse effect. However it is by far the most active GHG: its level of concentration increases even more rapidly than that of CO_2. Among the principal sources of methane emissions are landfills, paddy-rice fields, livestock breeding and burning of agricultural waste.

Sources: OECD, UNO, UNEP

The future of waste is its disappearance

Find out more

Only 20% of the waste produced in the world today is treated.

➤ *Industrial pollution and disasters*
Urban environment

The Basel Convention

The European Union as well as 135 individual countries have ratified the Basel Convention. The United States is one of the countries which have not signed.

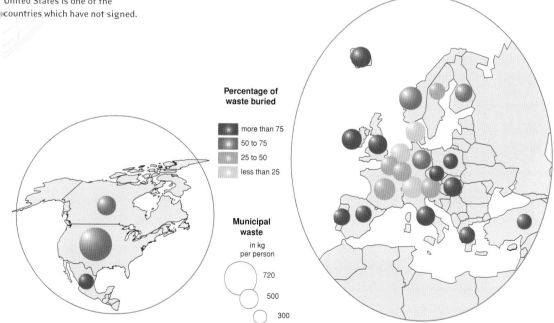

Percentage of
waste buried

more than 75
50 to 75
25 to 50
less than 25

Municipal
waste
in kg
per person

720

500

300

Municipal waste in OECD countries

One third of total investment in combating pollution is earmarked for management and treatment of municipal waste, even if this type of waste represents only a small percentage of total waste production. Accelerated economic growth means there is more waste to dispose of: in OECD countries between 1980 and the end of the 1990s, municipal waste production increased by 40% to 500 kg per person... and OECD countries anticipate 70% to 100% further growth in their GDP. Most waste in OECD countries is simply sent to landfill; if it is treated at all, the method most frequently used is incineration.

Urban Environment

By 2025 the world's total urban population will have doubled, reaching 5 billion (six of every 10 human beings). The basic needs of these new urban dwellers must be met. In many cases they have fled to the city to escape poverty, natural disasters or conflicts.

Cities are of course centres of economic development - melting pots where important cultural and social exchanges take place. Developing countries' revenues are already mainly produced in urban centers. Seoul's GDP is greater than that of all Indonesia. Most urban populations have better access to health care and education. However cities also generate exclusion, inequality, and loss of solidarity.

The problems that accompany uncontrolled development are concentrated in most urban areas. These include uncollected refuse, congestion, atmospheric pollution, lack of sanitation, social malaise and exclusion, and insecurity.

In 1996, at the United Nations Conference on Human Settlements (Habitat) in Istanbul, it was estimated that 1 billion people worldwide did not have a suitable place to live and that over 100 million were homeless. In many countries WHO has been able to demonstrate a connection between unhealthy living conditions and criminality.

The international community is becoming increasingly aware of the human, social and political risks presented by urban concentrations - risks for which neither inhabitants nor local authorities are prepared. In a number of developing countries these authorities do not have the political or financial means to meet even the most basic needs, such as drinking water, sanitation and electricity. In Asia only 3% of public funding is set aside for management by local communities, compared with an average of 40% in industrialized countries.

Access to basic necessities for the most disadvantaged, the struggle against poverty, and social integration should be based on enhancement of the power of local authorities, and on sustainable development strategies. A number of communities are putting Local Agenda 21s into place these are action plans for the 21st century elaborated and implemented in collaboration with local populations.

Nitrogen oxides

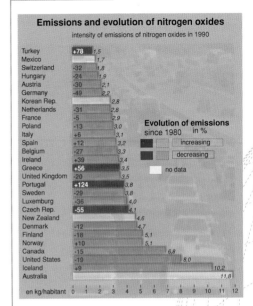

One of the effects of urbanisation is increased automobile traffic, which produces nitrogen oxides, among the main causes of air pollution.

Megalopolis populations
in millions

Find out more

6,500 urban communities established Agenda 21s offices in 2001

▶ Demography
Access to water
Transport
Inequality and poverty

By 2025 half the people living in cities will be in developing countries (compared with 25% in 1995)

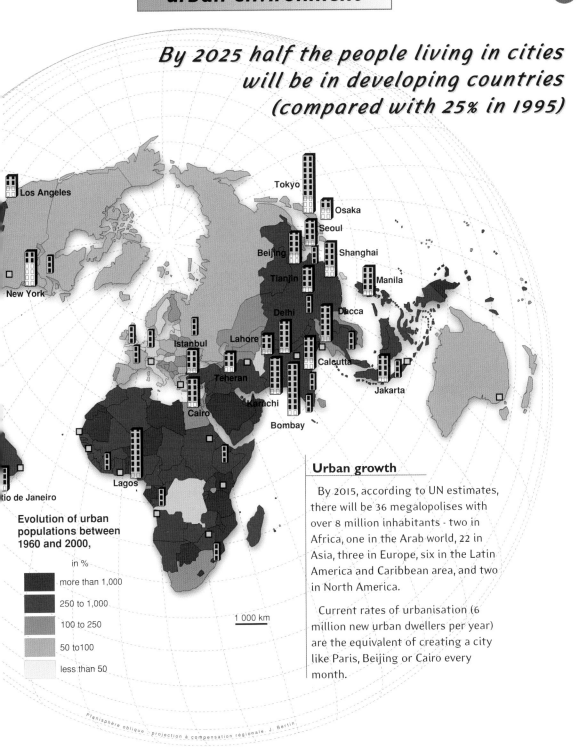

Tokyo
Los Angeles
Osaka
Seoul
Beijing
Shanghai
New York
Tianjin
Manila
Delhi
Dacca
Istanbul
Lahore
Calcutta
Teheran
Karachi
Jakarta
Cairo
Bombay
Lagos
Rio de Janeiro

Urban growth

By 2015, according to UN estimates, there will be 36 megalopolises with over 8 million inhabitants - two in Africa, one in the Arab world, 22 in Asia, three in Europe, six in the Latin America and Caribbean area, and two in North America.

Current rates of urbanisation (6 million new urban dwellers per year) are the equivalent of creating a city like Paris, Beijing or Cairo every month.

Evolution of urban populations between 1960 and 2000,

in %

- more than 1,000
- 250 to 1,000
- 100 to 250
- 50 to100
- less than 50

1 000 km

Planisphère oblique : projection à compensation régionale J. Bertin

Sources: CIA, OMS, ONU

49

Ecological footprint

Demographic changes, exploitation and pro-duction technologies, greenhouse gas emissions, waste generated by transport, agriculture and consumption all have impacts on the environ-ment. Measuring these impacts is difficult. The ecological footprint, an indicator proposed by the WWF (World Wide Fund for Nature), pro-vides an estimation, per surface unit and per inhabitant, of the pressure human activities put on the planet's ecosystems.

This footprint is calculated based on data published by United Nations agencies and by the UN's intergovernmental group of scientific experts on climatic change. Six categories of human activity are measured:

* infrastructure intended for lodging, trans-port, industrial production and hydraulic power production;

* fossil fuel combustion producing atmosphe-ric emissions of CO_2;

* productive fishing zones (about 3.2 billion hectares);

* exploitation of natural or planted forests (about 3.3 billion hectares);

* livestock production on pasture and forest land (about 4.6 billion hectares);

* cultivation (about 1.3 billion hectares of crop land).

Natural capital is not inexhaustible. This indica-tor shows that exploitation, production and consumption are over 30% above the capacity of the planet's natural resources to renew them-selves and to absorb pollution. Without a radi-cal change of direction, this global over-consump-tion will lead to the impoverishment of the enti-re planet.

GDP is not the only indicator of development. The ecological footprint suggests the ecological challenges society faces if it is to preserve the resources that are indispensable to the welfare of present and future generations - and trans-form growth into sustainable development.

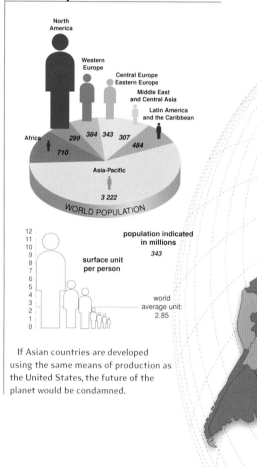

Wide disparities between continents

North America

Western Europe

Central Europe
Eastern Europe

Middle East and Central Asia

Latin America and the Caribbean

Africa   299   384   343   307

710   484

Asia-Pacific

3 222

WORLD POPULATION

population indicated in millions

343

surface unit per person

world average unit: 2.85

If Asian countries are developed using the same means of production as the United States, the future of the planet would be condamned.

Find out more

To ensure the continuation of the European fish industry, exploitation of fishing resources should reduced by 40%.

➤ *Seas and oceans*
Forests
Biodiversity
Climate change
Water withdrawal
Energy production and consumption

ecological footprint

Human activities have ecological impacts at least 30% beyond the planet's capacity to renew itself and absorb pollution

Surface unit per person, 1996

- 6 or more
- 4 to 6
- 2 to 4
- 1 to 2
- less than 1

1 000 km

Ecological footprints by country

The map shows the enormous disparities between developed and developing countries. Many African countries put little pressure on the planet's resources due to low water and energy consumption levels and lack of development. Hong Kong and the United States, on the other hand, consume resources well beyond their biological capacity.

Planisphère oblique : projection à compensation régionale. J. Bertin

Source: WWF

Should the Earth be seen as a vast financial playing field profiting a small minority, or a source of natural resources to be shared equitably? Sustainable development paves the way for a humanitarian and rational form of progress - the socially responsible exploitation of the natural resources that are our common heritage. It proclaims the need to fight inequality, to anticipate conflicts, and to preserve the planet - for a sustainable community.

Economy, Dependency and Solidarity

Water withdrawal

Fewer than 10 countries possess 60% of the world's available fresh water supply: Brazil (5,670 km³/year), Russia (3,904), China (2,880), Canada (2,850), Indonesia (2,530), the United States (2,478), India (1,150), Colombia (1,112) and Zaire (1,020). On the other hand, a number of arid countries (e.g. Cyprus, Jordan, Libya, Singapore, Malta) suffer from "water stress".

Natural water resources are made up of ancient supplies - the term "fossil water" may be used - or are produced through natural cycles. These resources may be renewable, but they are not inexhaustible. Intensive exploitation can dry up the aquifers that supply basic human needs.

Water consumption, which has increased sevenfold since the beginning of the 20th century, has doubled during the last 20 years - essentially for agricultural purposes, especially irrigation. Water exploitation is most intensive in countries where irrigation has long been essential (e.g. Iraq, Pakistan, Madagascar, Egypt, the Central Asian republics) and in countries where irrigation and high levels of public consumption have been combined, such as the United States, Spain, Argentina, Australia.

Increased water withdrawal is related to population growth, particularly in urban areas, and to greater water consumption per inhabitant globally, although wide disparities exist: in Ciudad Juarez (Mexico) average consumption is 285 litres per person, whereas across the border in El Paso (United States) the average is 750 litres, of which 50% is used for leisure activities (golf courses, swimming pools) and air conditioning.

Many areas have been severely damaged by excessive water withdrawal (e.g. the Aral Sea and the Everglades in Florida) and by industrial pollution. In several southern Mediterranean countries renewable water resources are almost completely exhausted (Egypt, Israel, Libya, Malta) or risk being exhausted during the 21st century (Algeria, Cyprus, the Palestinian West Bank, Tunisia).

Non-sustainable water exploitation

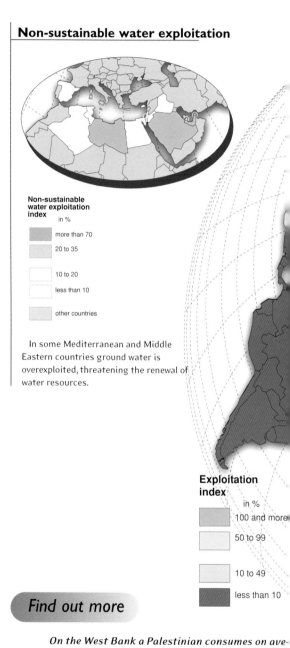

Non-sustainable water exploitation index in %

- more than 70
- 20 to 35
- 10 to 20
- less than 10
- other countries

In some Mediterranean and Middle Eastern countries ground water is overexploited, threatening the renewal of water resources.

Exploitation index in %

- 100 and more
- 50 to 99
- 10 to 49
- less than 10

Find out more

On the West Bank a Palestinian consumes on average 70 litres of water per day and an Israeli 260 litres.

➤ *Access to water*
Ecological footprint

On average Americans consume 600 litres of water per day, Europeans 250 and Africans 30

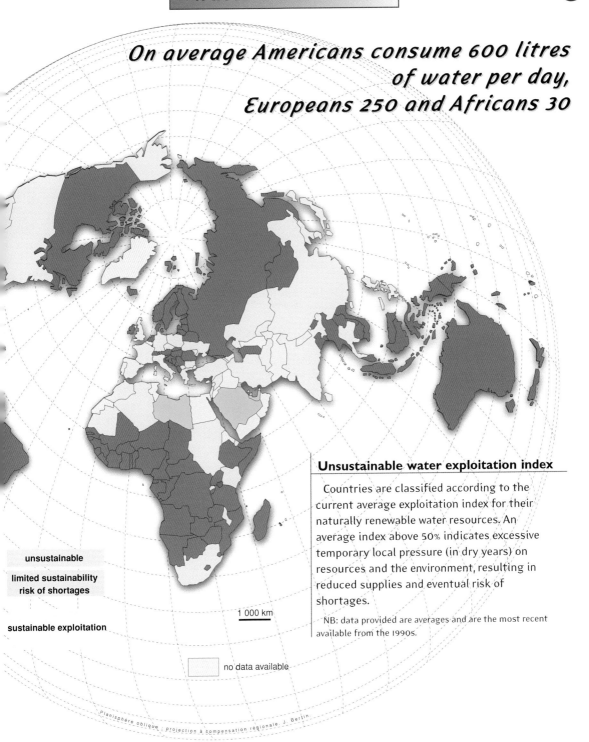

Unsustainable water exploitation index

Countries are classified according to the current average exploitation index for their naturally renewable water resources. An average index above 50% indicates excessive temporary local pressure (in dry years) on resources and the environment, resulting in reduced supplies and eventual risk of shortages.

NB: data provided are averages and are the most recent available from the 1990s.

unsustainable

limited sustainability
risk of shortages

1 000 km

sustainable exploitation

no data available

Planisphère oblique : projection à compensation régionale. J. Berlin.

Sources: *Aquastat-FAO, Plan Bleu (Jean Margat), UNEP*

Energy
production and consumption

Predicted energy demand in 2020 would have catastrophic effects in terms of climate change and pollution. If sustainable development is to become a reality, global energy use needs to be shared equitably, with industrialized countries reducing their consumption so developing countries can increase theirs. Access to energy is essential for economic development, elimination of poverty, and provision of the most basic human necessities including food, heating, lighting and access to information.

This enormous challenge requires immediate solutions with respect to the many populations that do not enjoy the comforts long taken for granted in developed countries. Energy-related risks should be eliminated without delay. Thus energy consumption needs to fall at the same time as polluting and dangerous energy sources are restricted.

Oil continues to be the most popular energy source globally. Consumption of gas, which has been on the increase, is now almost as great as that of coal. Use of hydroelectricity and other renewable sources is also increasing, but has had little impact so far on overall growth in energy demand. The nuclear industry, which has been rejected in a number of countries, is still far from capable of adequately addressing the problem of nuclear waste. Nuclear energy consumption will probably stabilize by the year 2020.

Since the 1997 Kyoto Protocol on climate change was agreed, the international commu-

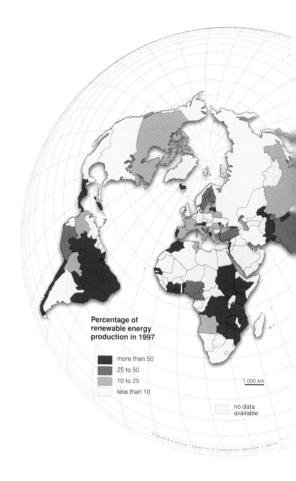

Percentage of renewable energy production in 1997

- more than 50
- 25 to 50
- 10 to 25
- less than 10
- no data available

1 000 km

nity has become increasingly aware of the effects of CO_2 emissions related to transport, heating, industry and agriculture.

Energy control is a priority for sustainable development. To achieve it, we need energy efficiency programmes and greater use of renewables, application of the polluter-pays principle (especially in the transport sector) and widespread public information campaigns.

Sources: IEA, World Bank, OECD

energy production and consumption

Unless energy policies change, global energy demand will increase by 65% between 1995 and 2020

Find out more

Over 2 billion people have no access to electricity.

► Desertification
Forests
Climate change
Transport

Renewable energy

Wind and solar power represent only 11.5% of current energy production. Hydroelectricity, which produced 14% of total electricity in OECD countries in 1999, is the most significant renewable energy source.

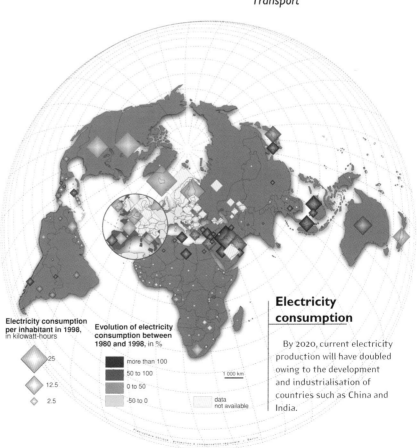

Electricity consumption

By 2020, current electricity production will have doubled owing to the development and industrialisation of countries such as China and India.

Electricity consumption per inhabitant in 1998, in kilowatt-hours

◇ 25
◇ 12.5
◇ 2.5

Evolution of electricity consumption between 1980 and 1998, in %

more than 100
50 to 100
0 to 50
-50 to 0
data not available

1 000 km

Agriculture

By 2020, the planet's population will have reached 8 billion. Nearly 70% of the population will live in cities. Even today the basic food needs of 2 billion people in the world are not being met by agriculture. The poorest countries do not produce enough to feed their own populations, nor do they have the means to supply their needs through imports. The development of sustainable agriculture capable of providing a solution to these problems is a challenge of great environmental, economic and human significance.

Crop yields will of course have to be increased, but without damaging soil quality, water resources or genetic diversity. Systematic recourse to agro-chemistry (fertilizers, insecticides, fungicides) has degraded natural habitats in several of the world's regions. The giants of the agro-chemical industry advocate GMOs - manipulating seeds' genetic formula - notably because this reinforces the organism's disease resistance. Precaution seems particularly relevant in the case of GMOs. Can one take the risk of developing a technology without knowing what the real impact on health and the environment may be?

Agriculture is among the global problems which must be addressed at local level. The great majority of developing countries cannot participate in the global market because the rules of the game have been perverted through subsidization of farmers in industrialized countries. Moreover, the most technical and sophisticated conception of agriculture presents many dangers. The emphasis should be on agricultural proximity and autonomy of food supply, especially in the case of cities, where there are the most mouths to feed. 800 million urban dwellers (between one quarter and two thirds of urban households) are already involved in urban agriculture.

Today the international community must address a number of pressing issues: meeting the food requirements of current and future generations, protecting the environment and genetic diversity, introducing sustainable development of the planet's resources, and increasing developing countries' production capacity and access to the global market.

GMOs

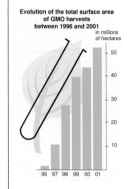

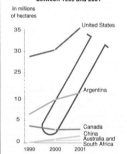

In 2001, GMO crops worldwide were grown on over 50 million hectares, 70% of which were in the United States. Other producing countries are Argentina, Canada, China and Brazil.

Find out more

Just fifteen crops provide the world with 90% of its foodstuffs. Three of them - rice, wheat and corn - are the staple diet of 4 billion people.

▶ *Malnutrition*
Biodiversity
Water withdrawal

Cereal production will have to be increased by 40% before 2025 to meet food demand

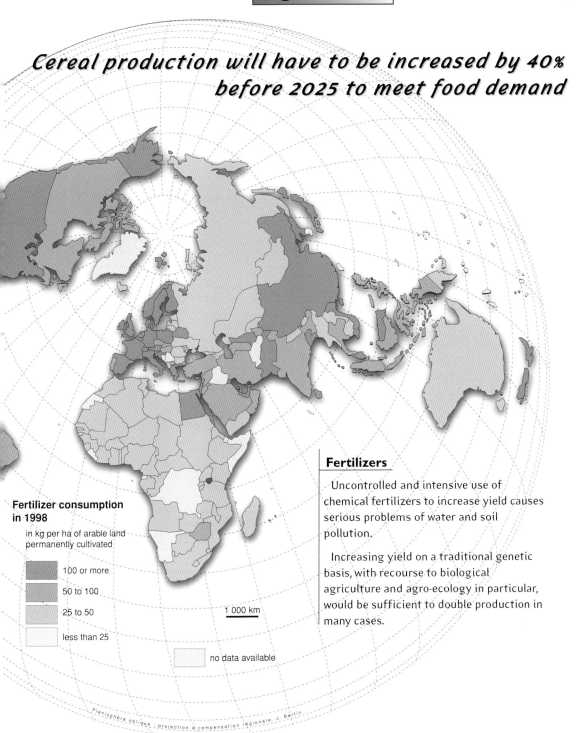

Fertilizers

Uncontrolled and intensive use of chemical fertilizers to increase yield causes serious problems of water and soil pollution.

Increasing yield on a traditional genetic basis, with recourse to biological agriculture and agro-ecology in particular, would be sufficient to double production in many cases.

Fertilizer consumption in 1998

in kg per ha of arable land permanently cultivated

- 100 or more
- 50 to 100
- 25 to 50
- less than 25

no data available

1 000 km

Planisphère oblique : Projection à compensation régionale. J. Bertin.

Sources: FAO, ISAAA

59

Transport

Transport contributes to autonomy and development on both personal and economic levels. Many developing countries legitimately aspire to the freedom promised by transport. However growing demand worldwide has led to an explosion in the number of cars on the road, as wells as increases in energy consumption and in emissions which are harmful to health and the environment. According to the World Health Organization, pollution related to transport is responsible for 500,000 deaths and 4 to 5 million cases of chronic bronchitis per year.

Air and ground transport not only cause health and environmental damage but also consumes energy. Transport currently uses up one quarter of global energy, and consumption in developing countries is increasing by 5% a year. Automobiles burn one third of the petrol produced in the world.

The International Union for Public Transport (IUPT) has studied the effectiveness of transport policies in 100 cities (60 in developed countries and 40 in countries in transition or developing countries). Assessment of these policies was based on 200 indicators (e.g. how well users are served, economic viability, pollution control). Two major factors can be shown to determine the quality of urban transport policies:

* regional development, bearing in mind that urban expansion increases dependence on the automobile and swallows up an important portion of consumer and community budgets;

* provision of public transport, including in peripheral zones, as public transport is unquestionably

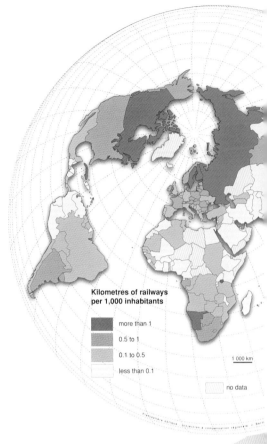

Kilometres of railways per 1,000 inhabitants

- more than 1
- 0.5 to 1
- 0.1 to 0.5
- less than 0.1
- no data

1,000 km

much the best option in terms of energy and environment.

Even if automotive manufacturers have made progress in reducing pollutant emissions and have promised us clean vehicles in the future (especially through development of battery-powered engines), cities are certain to become "unbreathable" and dangerous unless governments and communities take strong action in favour of public transport.

If China...

In Switzerland two thirds of the population (65%) owns a car. If, during the development process, the Chinese "legitimately" asserted their right to have an equivalent fleet, the total number of vehicles operating in the world would almost double. The planet would have to set aside two thirds of its petrol for private vehicles, and there would be twice the amount of CO_2 emissions!

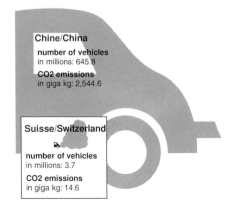

Chine/China

number of vehicles in millions: 645.8

CO2 emissions in giga kg: 2,544.6

Suisse/Switzerland

number of vehicles in millions: 3.7

CO2 emissions in giga kg: 14.6

Automobile pollution kills more people than road accidents in Austria, France and Switzerland

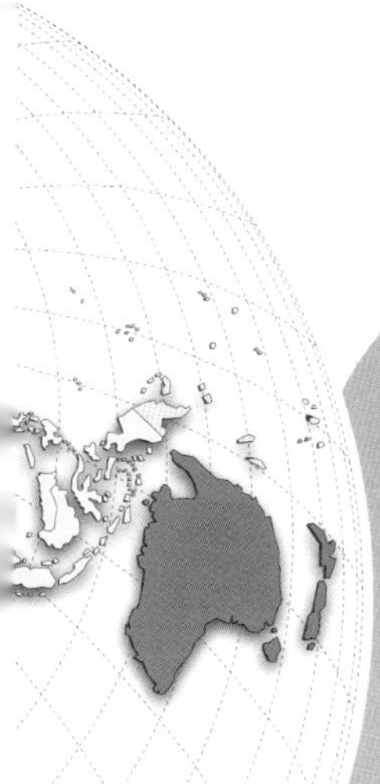

Find out more

Cars consume four times as much more energy per passenger as public transport.

Railways

As long as their environmental impacts are controlled, railways are an excellent alternative to road transport - especially for carrying freight. But in developing countries, where they are one of the most accessible types of transport, railways are still far from being able to meet all mobility needs.

▶ *Climate change*
Urban environment
Energy production
and consumption

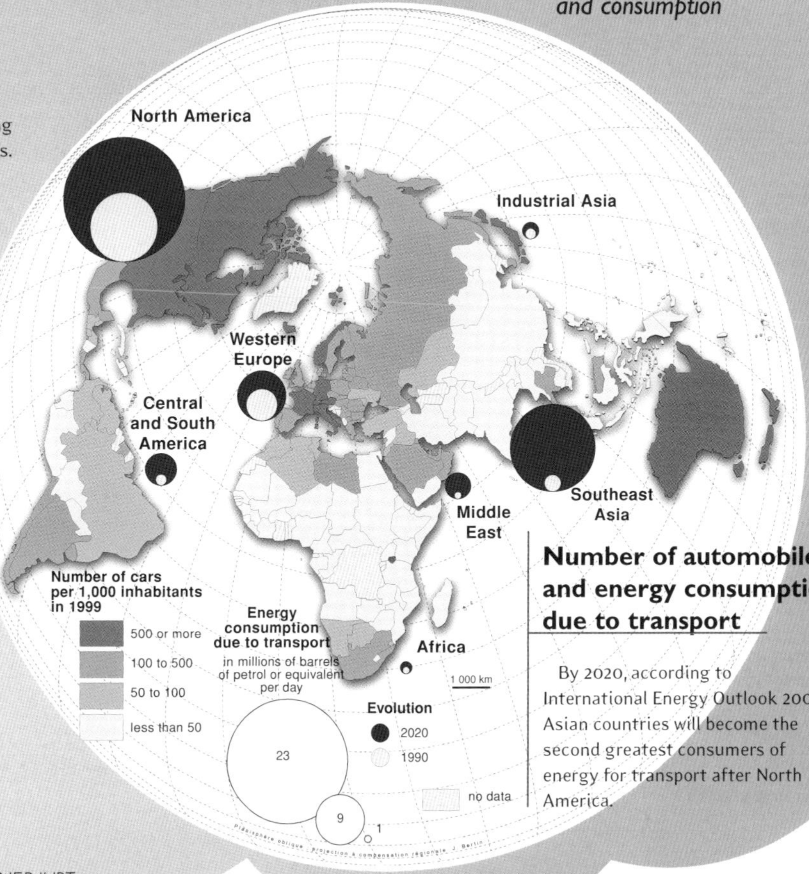

Air pollution

A growing number of countries are implementing regulations concerned with measuring atmospheric pollutants, so that they can inform and alert the public about health risks and (when pollution peaks) ban or restrict automobile use.

North America

Industrial Asia

Western Europe

Central and South America

Middle East

Southeast Asia

Number of cars per 1,000 inhabitants in 1999

- 500 or more
- 100 to 500
- 50 to 100
- less than 50

Energy consumption due to transport
in millions of barrels of petrol or equivalent per day

Africa

Number of automobiles and energy consumption due to transport

By 2020, according to International Energy Outlook 2001, Asian countries will become the second greatest consumers of energy for transport after North America.

Evolution
- 2020
- 1990

23

no data

1 000 km

9 1

urces: IEA, IAC, WHO, UNDP, UNEP, IUPT

Communication

Access to information, and free exchanges and communications, are essential for people to be able to play an active role in society and participate politically. Whereas access to telephone networks is improving globally (and has widely developed due to the mobile telephone explosion), in many countries most people still do not have Internet access.

There is growing evidence of inequality with respect to Internet use. The network spread incredibly quickly - in just four years over 50 million people were connected, while it took the telephone 75 years to achieve the same figures. However a closer look at the map reveals deep disparities. Over 65% of available servers are in the United States and Canada and 22% are in Europe, compared with 0.3% in Africa.

Once again, Africa has been left behind with respect to access to information and social interaction. For Africans, the Internet is accessible only through associations, community centres, schools and private shops offering communication systems.

Yet the telecommunications sector, particularly its virtual office opportunities, could provide a very positive alternative environmentally if it were available to all. Virtual offices are a solution to the harmful effects of overcrowded cities and classic communication networks: e.g. traffic congestion, cramped city centres, stress, pollution and health risks.

The World Conference on Development and Telecommunications (Istanbul, March 2002) emphasized the importance of reducing the "digital fracture" which is broadening the gulf of inequality, particularly in regard to access to learning, education, and freedom of expression. Lack of necessary infrastructure and of government impetus obstructs Internet implementation even more than the cost of equipment. The United Nations has launched a plan of action for December 2003 in Geneva. To be continued...

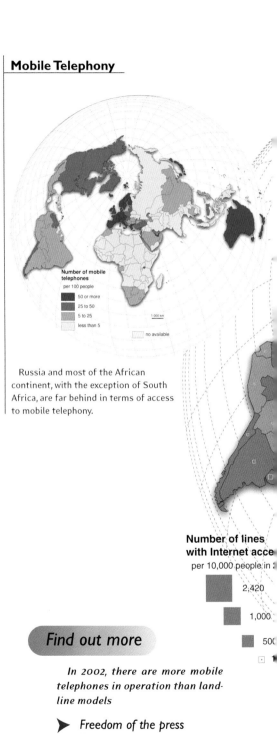

Mobile Telephony

Number of mobile telephones
per 100 people

- 50 or more
- 25 to 50
- 5 to 25
- less than 5
- no available

1 000 km

Russia and most of the African continent, with the exception of South Africa, are far behind in terms of access to mobile telephony.

Number of lines with Internet acce
per 10,000 people in 2

- 2,420
- 1,000
- 50(

Find out more

In 2002, there are more mobile telephones in operation than landline models

➤ Freedom of the press
Transport

One out of six people on the planet owns a mobile telephone

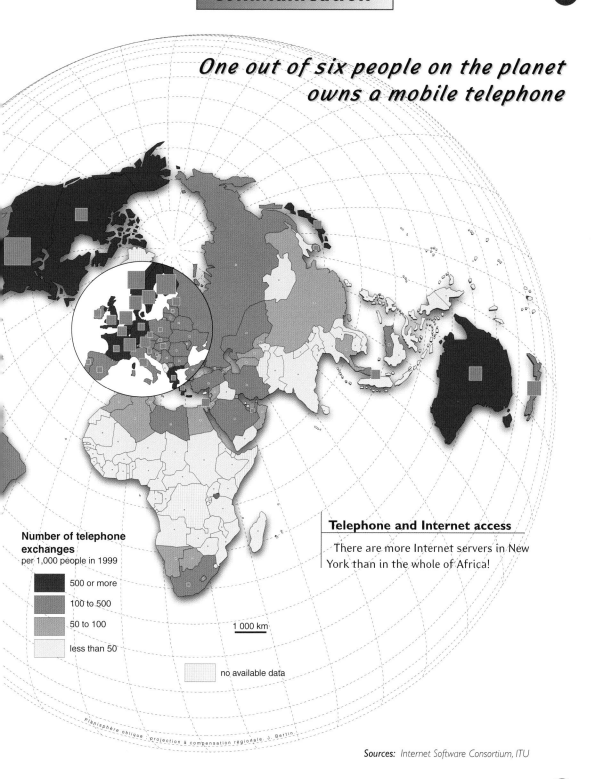

Number of telephone exchanges
per 1,000 people in 1999

- 500 or more
- 100 to 500
- 50 to 100
- less than 50

no available data

1 000 km

Telephone and Internet access

There are more Internet servers in New York than in the whole of Africa!

Planisphère oblique ; projection à compensation régionale ; J. Bertin.

Sources: *Internet Software Consortium, ITU*

Inequality and poverty

Reducing inequality and the gap between rich and poor countries was one of the priorities of the Rio Earth Summit. Ten years later, no progress has been made.

In 1971, 27 countries had a per capita GNP of below 900 dollars a year; 49 countries are in a comparable situation today, and 34 of these countries are in Africa. Of the planet's 6 billion people, 1.2 billion live on less than one dollar per day and 2.4 billion on less than two dollars a day. At the other extreme, 80% of the world's wealth is in the hands of 15% of the people who live in the richest countries.

The gap has not ceased to widen between the rich countries and the poor countries and continents which have experienced little development: e.g. Sub-Saharan Africa, North Korea, Myanmar or Afghanistan. In 1970, average earnings in Sub-Saharan Africa were about 12 times less than in rich countries. Today they are 20 times less.

In six of the poorest African countries (Botswana, Burundi, Namibia, Rwanda, Zambia and Zimbabwe) the AIDS epidemic has shortened life expectancy by seven years. It has reduced the number of able-bodied workers, which has begun to affect crop production and is leading towards even greater poverty. Thus it will become impossible to purchase needed medications. Most of these countries also face serious internal crises such as corruption and civil war, further impeding development.

Poverty, like external debt, is part of a vicious circle. In particular, it causes capital flight: 40% of Africa's resources are invested outside the continent: resources that are indispensable at home, but instead will yield a profit elsewhere.

Inequality within countries is also a growing cause for concern. Accelerated growth in China, India and Indonesia has undoubtedly improved national GNP, but it has also widened the gulf between the living standards of inhabitants in cities and rural areas.

Inequality has increased over the last ten years in the most industrialized countries: levels of unemployment have soared, leading to precarious living conditions, while some governments have begun to

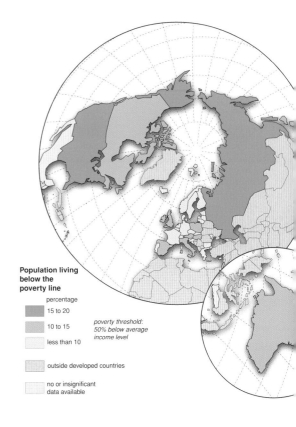

Population living below the poverty line

percentage

- 15 to 20
- 10 to 15
- less than 10

poverty threshold: 50% below average income level

- outside developed countries
- no or insignificant data available

question the viability of social protection systems introduced at the end of the Second World war.

Market forces on their own produce inequality within countries and globally. Government intervention is more essential than ever, along with the consolidation of systems of national and international solidarity.

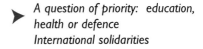

Find out more

In the United States 1% of the population controls 38% of the country's wealth.

▶ *A question of priority: education, health or defence*
International solidarities

inequality and poverty

1.2 billion people live on less than one dollar per day

Wide gaps between the rich and the poor

Poverty in developed countries

In the United States, as in Russia, over 16% of the population lives below the poverty line. This threshold, determined by the countries themselves, is calculated at 50% below the average income level.

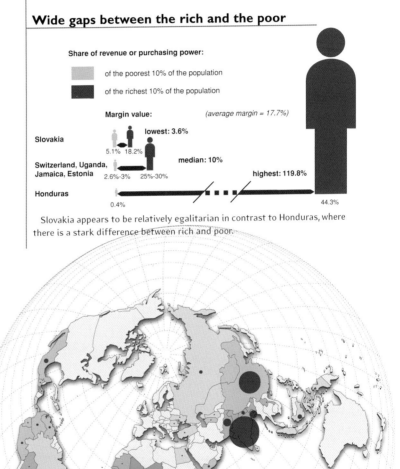

Share of revenue or purchasing power:

- of the poorest 10% of the population
- of the richest 10% of the population

Margin value: *(average margin = 17.7%)*

Slovakia
lowest: 3.6%
5.1% 18.2%

Switzerland, Uganda, Jamaica, Estonia
median: 10%
2.6%-3%   25%-30%

Honduras
highest: 119.8%
0.4%   44.3%

Slovakia appears to be relatively egalitarian in contrast to Honduras, where there is a stark difference between rich and poor.

Absolute poverty

Of course poverty is exists throughout Africa, China and India. Data on extreme poverty, however, are unavailable for many countries.

Number of people living on less than $1 per day,
in millions
425
80
10
1

Percentage of the population living on less than $1 per day
- 50 and more
- 25 to 50
- 10 to 25
- less than 10
- no or insignificant data available

1 000 km

Source: World Bank

Dependency

Economists would never question the principle of investment, as it plays an essential role in the global economy. Loans by private banks and international financial institutions (the World Bank, IMF) allow countries, whether rich or poor, to finance development projects.

When a country's available revenue is below required repayment costs, debt can become part of a never-ending downward spiral. Some two thirds of the least advanced countries (LACs) face unrealistic debt charges compared with their financial capacity, forcing the poorest of them to curb development projects. Incapable of meeting reimbursement deadlines, they accumulate payment arrears or even contract new loans to pay the interest on their debt. Most throw all their resources into repayment, neglecting essential expenditure on health, education and poverty alleviation. Over a period of ten years debt in developing countries increased by 34%, to a total of 2, 500 billion dollars in 2000.

A growing number of individuals and organizations that are calling for solidarity challenge the legitimacy of the debt with which poor countries are burdened, suspecting financial institutions of making them pay inflated amounts for debt servicing. According to the World Bank, between 1980 and 2000 Latin American countries paid 15.4 billion dollars in interest to the IMF. In July 2000, after eighteen years of proceedings, the Federal Tribunal in Buenos Aires declared the Argentinean debt illegal and found the IMF, private creditors and the Federal Reserve Bank of the United States culpable.

A movement emerging from NGOs such as ATTAC (Association for the Taxation of Financial Transactions for the Aid of Citizens) and public cooperation organizations calls for cancelling the debt of the poorest countries or converting it into sustainable development

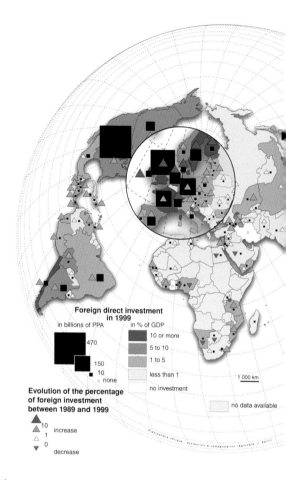

Foreign direct investment in 1999

in billions of PPA

470
150
10
□ none

in % of GDP
■ 10 or more
5 to 10
1 to 5
less than 1
no investment
no data available

1 000 km

Evolution of the percentage of foreign investment between 1989 and 1999

▲ 10
▲ 1   increase
△ 1
△ 0
▼ 0   decrease

programmes. The obstacles continually encountered during negotiations reveal the strength of resistance within developed countries and international financial institutions.

In certain developing countries corruption aggravates the debt question, as aid is diverted into the hands of the power elite.

The consequences of debt are multiple and serious. They include the "brain drain" and threats to peace and security. International financial institutions and governments have an obligation to take responsibility for solidarity between rich and poor countries, as well as to ensure that public spending commitments to development are respected and that the struggle against corruption continues.

Sources: ATTAC, World Bank, OECD

The poorest countries are prisoners of a debt trap

Find out more

150 million African children live below
the poverty threshold.

➤ Conflict
Corruption
International solidarities

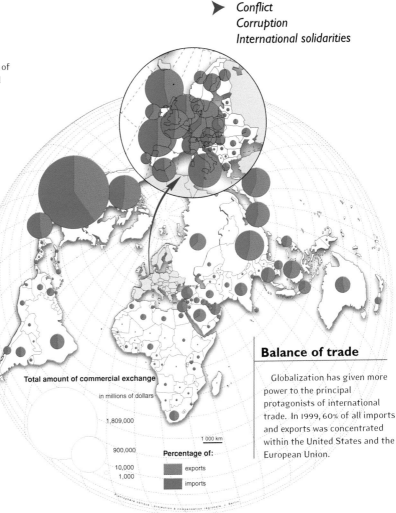

Direct investment abroad

Direct investment in developing
countries continues to be the source of
much debate within the international
community. The flux towards such
countries, particularly Africa, is
continually retreating.

Debt in Africa

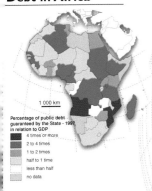

1 000 km

Percentage of public debt
guaranteed by the State - 1997
in relation to GDP
- 4 times or more
- 2 to 4 times
- 1 to 2 times
- half to 1 time
- less than half
- no data

Democracy and peace continue
to be the cornerstones of
development and debt control.
Governments in some African
countries swallow up public
resources in their military
budgets. For most of these
countries, however, the debt is
chronic. Extreme poverty,
epidemics, and banishment from
global markets make it impossible
for them to resolve their debts.

Total amount of commercial exchange

in millions of dollars

1,809,000

900,000

10,000
1,000

1 000 km

Percentage of:
- exports
- imports

Balance of trade

Globalization has given more
power to the principal
protagonists of international
trade. In 1999, 60% of all imports
and exports was concentrated
within the United States and the
European Union.

67

Corruption

Corruption is rife in the North and South: contracts for arms and for petrol exploitation are won through bribery, political campaigns are financed clandestinely, public funds are embezzled, money is laundered in collusion with banks, and tax havens abound.

The Maxwell group's downfall in 1991 is a well-known example of corruption: 738 million euros was stolen from the employees' pension fund, leading to the company's ruin. More recently, the bankruptcy of the American corporation Enron has sown doubts on all international stock markets about the reliability of company accounting practices.

Transparency International, an association which currently exists in eighty countries, has established a Corruption Perception Index (CPI) based on information gathered mainly from the media and NGOs. This index classifies countries according to their level of corruption.

The OECD Convention on fighting corruption, in effect since 1999, reflects the first signs of institutional awareness of this phenomenon. It calls for greater vigilance by member countries with respect to transparency in public affairs and reinforcement of companies' internal controls. The European Union has made cooperation in this area a condition for adhesion by Central and Eastern European countries.

Companies also have an essential role to play in promoting financial transparency. The World Business Council for Sustainable Development network brings together one hundred global groups, such as Suez or ST Microelectronics, which have agreed that fighting corruption is one of the indicators of sustainable development. Certain ethical funds (which take into account stock market performance, but also social and environmental commitments) do not include companies suspected of corruption in their portforlios.

Freedom of the press, consumer decision-making, and shareholder investment choices are increasingly effective ways to combat "dirty money".

Money laundering

23 countries are on the "black list" for refusing to participate in the fight against money laundering

as of 27 February 2002

Andorra
Anguilla
Bahamas
Belize
Dominica
Gibraltar
Cook Islands
Marshall Islands
Turks and Caicos Islands
American Virgin Islands
British Virgin Islands
Liberia
Liechtenstein
Maldives
Monaco
Montserrat
Nauru
Niue
Panama
St. Lucia
St. Kitts and Nevis
Samoa
Vanuatu

The only way to resolve the problem of dirty money would be for the international community to isolate countries that harbour drug and arms trafficking and to impose sanctions.

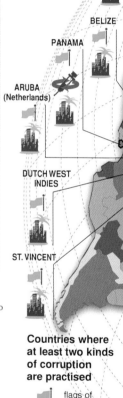

BAHAMA

BELIZE

PANAMA

ARUBA
(Netherlands)

DUTCH WEST
INDIES

ST. VINCENT

Countries where at least two kinds of corruption are practised

flags of convenience

drug trafficking

tax havens

prejudiced fiscal practice

Find out more

Ethical funds account for 2,000 billion dollars in United States.

▶ *Freedom of the press*
Dependency
International solidarities

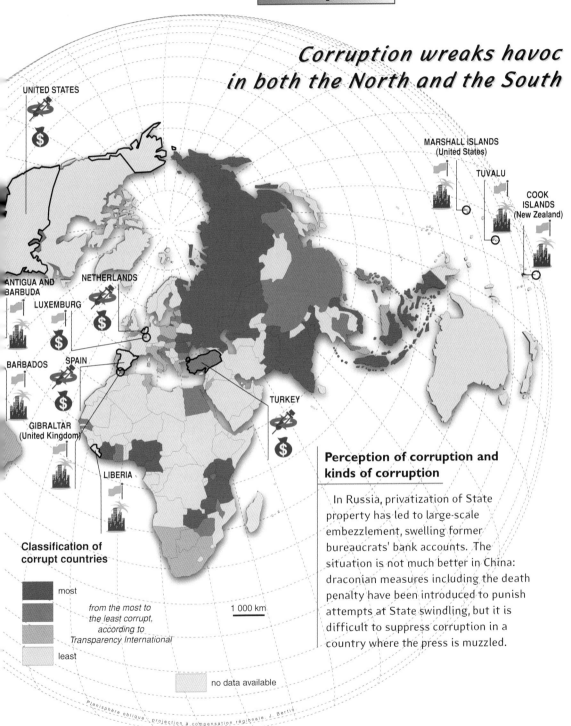

Corruption wreaks havoc in both the North and the South

UNITED STATES

MARSHALL ISLANDS
(United States)

TUVALU

COOK
ISLANDS
(New Zealand)

ANTIGUA AND
BARBUDA

NETHERLANDS

LUXEMBURG

BARBADOS

SPAIN

TURKEY

GIBRALTAR
(United Kingdom)

LIBERIA

**Classification of
corrupt countries**

most

from the most to
the least corrupt,
according to
Transparency International

least

no data available

1 000 km

Perception of corruption and kinds of corruption

In Russia, privatization of State property has led to large-scale embezzlement, swelling former bureaucrats' bank accounts. The situation is not much better in China: draconian measures including the death penalty have been introduced to punish attempts at State swindling, but it is difficult to suppress corruption in a country where the press is muzzled.

Planisphère oblique – projection à compensation régionale J. Bertin

Sources: European Commission, FATF, OECD, Transparency International, WBCSD

Public spending

Public spending indicates a country's priorities regarding more equitable redistribution of its wealth and solidarity with those most in need.

How to prioritise education, health and defence? Since 1990 the international community has given high priority to spending on universal education. Education is essential for development and for reducing inequality. It has positive effects on growth, environment and health - and it encourages members of civil society to participate actively in public decision making, which increases political stability.

In 2002 over 110 million children (60% of them girls) had no opportunity to obtain an education. European countries spend the equivalent of 5% of GDP on education (Denmark 8%, Greece 3.7%), but many other countries in the world have to spend much of their resources on debt repayment or are engaged in conflicts that entail heavy arms expenditure.

Access to health care is a matter of international as well as national solidarity. The World Health Organization has analysed public spending on health care in OECD countries. More resources are spent on health care in the United States than in any other country, but the US ranks 22nd in provision of quality health care to its citizens (there is considerable inequality between social classes, as well as between care provided in individual states). France ranks number one for health care quality and equality, although it is 12th in the spending category.

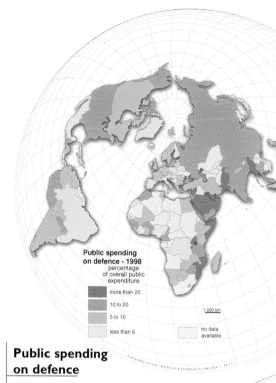

Public spending on defence - 1998
percentage of overall public expenditure

- more than 20
- 10 to 20
- 5 to 10
- less than 5

1 000 km

- no data available

Public spending on defence

Interpretation of data should take into account armed conflicts between 1990 and 1998. In this period the countries devoting the highest percentage of budgetary expenditure to defence were Somalia (38%), Saudi Arabia (36%) and Myanmar (36%). Pakistan topped the list in 2002, with 45% of its national budget earmarked for military expenditure.

Public spending on health care - 1998
percentage of total public expenditure

- more than 20
- 10 to 20
- 5 to 10
- less than 5

Find out more

Between 1996 and 2000, the G8 countries (the United States, Japan, Canada, France, Germany, the United Kingdom, Italy, Russia) were responsible for 87% of arms sales.

▶ *Access to education*
Conflict
International solidarities

Sources: *World Bank, WHO, SIPRI, UNES*

A question of priority: education, health or defence

In developing countries, military expenditure is extremely high, to the detriment of education and health care

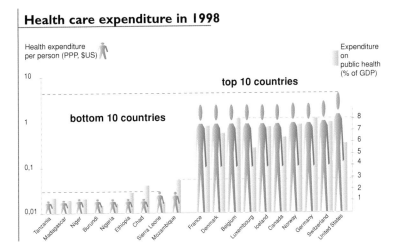

Health care expenditure in 1998

Health expenditure per person (PPP, $US)

Expenditure on public health (% of GDP)

bottom 10 countries

top 10 countries

Public spending on health care

The only way to ensure equal access to health care is through public spending. The governments of most OECD countries cover between 70% and 80% of total health expenditure. In countries like China, Lebanon or Nepal, where social solidarity is very limited, average coverage can be as little as 20%.

1 000 km

no data available

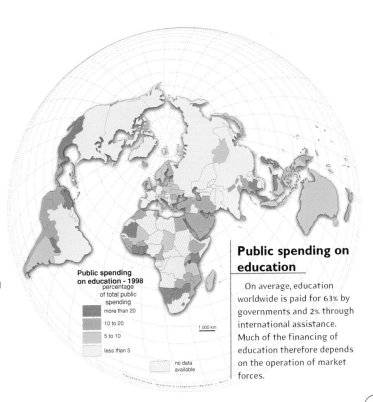

Public spending on education - 1998
percentage of total public spending

more than 20

10 to 20

5 to 10

less than 5

no data available

1 000 km

Public spending on education

On average, education worldwide is paid for 63% by governments and 2% through international assistance. Much of the financing of education therefore depends on the operation of market forces.

International Solidarities

Development assistance and contributions to the United Nations are the two principal means by which international solidarity is expressed.

In 1970, after former colonies in several parts of the world gained their independence, the UN General Assembly agreed (1) that developed countries should transfer financial resources to developing countries to help them become self-sufficient. An objective of 0.7% of gross national product (GNP) was established. At the Rio Earth Summit in 1992, governments were once again called upon to meet this objective.

It is mainly the OECD countries that provide development assistance, but they are still a long way from meeting this commitment. In 2000 they donated an average 0.22% of GNP (a total of 53.7 billion dollars). Some countries are considerably more generous than others: Denmark donates the equivalent of 1.06% of GNP, the United States only 0.10%. France has reduced its contribution by half since 1994. Only Denmark, Luxembourg, the Netherlands, Norway and Sweden have contributed more than 0.7%.

American aid to Africa fell from 1.9 billion dollars in 1993 to 933 million in 2000. Total aid to Sub-Saharan Africa from all donor countries fell from 32 dollars per person in 1990 to 19 dollars a decade later. This decrease in assistance coincides with the overwhelming indebtedness that makes it impossible for these countries to improve their economic situation.

Also under threat are contributions to the United Nations, which are another manifestation of international solidarity and the goal of sharing the world's wealth more equitably. Created in 1945, the UN is financed by contributions from its 185 members. Each country's contribution is calculated according to average income per inhabitant. These contributions are the organisation's only source of revenue. They finance peacekeeping operations (e.g. Blue

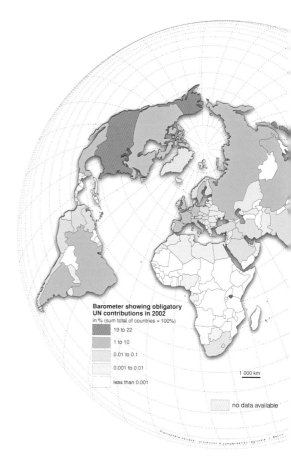

Barometer showing obligatory
UN contributions in 2002
in % (sum total of countries = 100%)

19 to 22
1 to 10
0.01 to 0.1
0.001 to 0.01
less than 0.001

1 000 km

no data available

Beret operations in Kosovo, Sierra Leone, East Timor and Congo) and UN agency missions intended to protect human rights, improve access to health care and education, and protect children.

In 2000, member states (2) owed over 3 billion dollars to the UN. The United States, the organisation's largest contributor (22% of the overall budget), was also the farthest in arrears. Although in 1999 it paid the minimum amount required to (just) avoid losing its right to vote, at the end of September 2000 it still owed 1.9 billion dollars.

1. Paragraph 43 of Resolution 2626.
2. The largest contributors were the United States, Japan, Germany, France, Italy, the United Kingdom, the Russian Federation, Canada, Spain, the Netherlands, Brazil, Australia, Sweden, Belgium and Argentina.

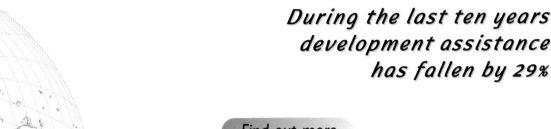

During the last ten years development assistance has fallen by 29%

Find out more

Only 1% of the UN's total budget, and a small part of development assistance, are earmarked for environmental protection.

➤ *Inequality and poverty*
Dependency

Obligatory contributions to the UN

The total UN budget for 2002-2003 is 2.6 billion dollars. The organisation's expenses are met by member states' obligatory contributions, based on their financial capacities (the minimum contribution was 0.001%, the maximum 22%). For the year 2002, 23% of the budget was allocated to regional and international development cooperation, 5% to human rights and humanitarian actions, and 2% to international law and justice.

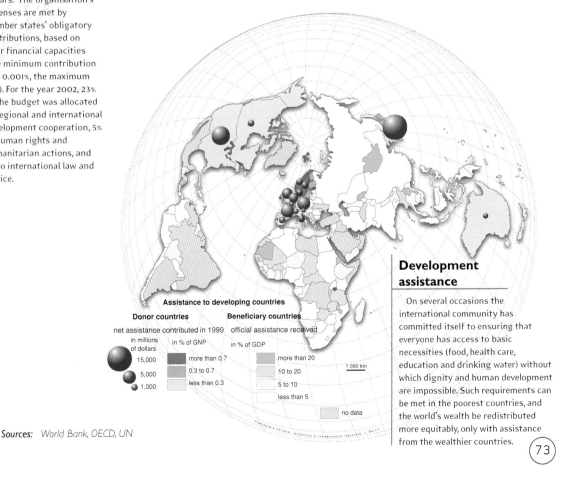

Assistance to developing countries

Donor countries

net assistance contributed in 1999
in millions of dollars

- 15,000
- 5,000
- 1,000

Beneficiary countries

official assistance received

in % of GNP
- more than 0.7
- 0.3 to 0.7
- less than 0.3

in % of GDP
- more than 20
- 10 to 20
- 5 to 10
- less than 5
- no data

1 000 km

Development assistance

On several occasions the international community has committed itself to ensuring that everyone has access to basic necessities (food, health care, education and drinking water) without which dignity and human development are impossible. Such requirements can be met in the poorest countries, and the world's wealth be redistributed more equitably, only with assistance from the wealthier countries.

Sources: World Bank, OECD, UN

Sustainable development: a social contract for the planet

The facts and figures in this Atlas seem to prove that humanity is stubbornly determined to self-destruct. While the future looks bleak, there are a few signs indicating that there could yet be light at the end of the tunnel

Probably the most important sign is the growth of citizens' movements and of independent networks providing information and expertise.

Owing to the repeated failure of existing institutions to combat poverty, pollution and risks, there has been a collective surge of innovation by local communities, experts and NGOs. They have developed networks of exchange and solidarity that constitute an alternative to the logic of domination and the process of self-destruction. NGOs in particular are essential participants in sustainable development. They are a driving force thanks to their continuous presence, their capacity to foresee social and environmental risks, and their unceasing vigilance.

The data presented here suggest the absolute necessity of strengthening such networks. It would be difficult to obtain data on corruption, sexual exploitation of children or poverty without the work of associations like Amnesty International and Transparency. Rarely do the governments concerned provide such information.

Organizations like Amnesty and Transparency are indispensable, as they make it possible to acquire the knowledge on which action can be based.

Since Rio, NGOs have become better aware of the need to coordinate demands that were previously separate (e.g. environmental protection, human rights, local solidarity, international cooperation) to reach wider audiences and increase opportunities for response. They have succeeded in gaining access to a growing share of the general public and of the press. If political leaders do not want to lose the support of the majority of their citizens, they can no longer ignore the network of exchange and solidarity developing around the issue of sustainable development.

In Africa, the desire for freedom of expression and social well-being has led to the formation of a multitude of associations, strengthening of the local press, mobilization of young people and women, and an end to the elite's hold on power. The vitality of civil society is capable of forming a barrier to dictatorship, injustice and corruption.

North America
22,224

Latin America and the Caribbean
577

Europe
2,395

Africa
654

Asia
1,471

Oceania
562

Number of NGOs

Another encouraging sign: the growing strength of local authorities and their engagement with social, economic and environmental issues.

Agenda 21, adopted at Rio, affirmed the determining role of local authorities in putting the principles of sustainable development into effect. Agenda 21 also encouraged elected representatives to work with local populations to design action programmes at the local level. It was with a view to actively supporting sustainable development that Local Agenda 21s began to be implemented.

Ten years after Rio, it can be seen that efforts to put sustainable development into effect have been most pertinent at the local level. Politicians are beginning to evaluate situations through direct consultation with local populations, and there is a more integral approach to environmental, social and economic issues. In some respects Local Agenda 21 activities function as laboratories for sustainable development: international institutions and decision-makers could eventually learn from them. Elected representatives are continually obliged to take or oversee decisions that have to meet the demands of local populations and prove their effectiveness in both the short and long term.

Local Agenda 21s are based on certain key elements which should not be disassociated:

- an inventory of the community's "state of affairs": what are the natural, ecological, cultural, industrial, economic, social, heritage and financial means at its disposition? What are its strong and weak points? Following such an analysis, how would investment be most beneficial to future progress?

- a conception of a "strategic project" for an area's development (the outcome of dialogue with local populations) that takes into account social, environmental and economic objectives;

- a definition of the means necessary to fulfil these objectives in progressive stages, mobilizing a population's "full human potential" to ensure success at every stage;

- regular evaluation of the results achieved, using standard indicators.

Is such an approach utopian? Yes, in that it its basis is a set of values rarely promoted in the political arena (e.g. long-term vision, a sense of responsibility, solidarity, transparency, evaluation). And no, in that a growing number of communities are successfully experimenting with this new method of exercising power through dialogue.

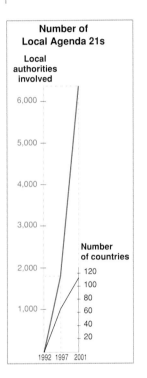

Number of Local Agenda 21s

Local authorities involved

Number of countries

While this movement may have taken some time to catch on, it has now succeeded in mobilizing networks in Northern as well as Southern cities, among them the International Council for Local Environmental Initiatives (ICLEI), the World Federation of United Cities (UTO), the Organization for Islamic Capitals and Cities (OICC), the MedCities network, and the Council of European Municipalities and Regions (CEMR). Local Agenda 21s had been initiated by 7,000 local groups in over 110 countries by the end of 2001.

The majority of Local Agenda 21s have been initiated in Europe, but the participatory methods increasingly used on other continents indicate the growing power of local democracy. In Asia and Africa such methods accompany a trend towards decentralization. In South America they encourage citizens to join the struggle against poverty and urban violence. Everywhere they reveal cities' potential to create a new kind of politics.

Not only have local authorities introduced innovative methods, but they also play a crucial role in resolving worldwide problems as part of decentralized cooperation or networks that include Healthy Cities (initiated by WHO), the World Alliance of Cities Against Poverty (supported by UNDP) and the Alliance of European Cities against Climate Change.

Still another sign: corporate environmental accounting and socially responsible investment ("ethical funds").

In 1999 the "Dow Jones Sustainability Indexes" were introduced; every year they assess the 2,000 companies with the greatest stock market capitalization (about 230 world groups). Together with the increasing amount of information made available by rating agencies specializing in sustainable development, these Sustainability Indexes have encouraged the development of "socially responsible investment".

Socially responsible investors evaluate companies in terms of financial criteria, but also environmental and social criteria (e.g. prevention of risk and pollution, respect for social norms, lack of racial or sexual discrimination, refusal to operate in totalitarian countries). Some sectors, such as weapons production, are also excluded. These funds, which have been as profitable as non-ethical ones, make it possible for investors to become directly involved in the sustainable development process. For example, they can influ-ence decision-making at shareholder meetings. Fifteen institutional investors in Mitsubishi have responded positively to demands by an

Number of local authorities that have established Local Agenda 21s, by geographical area

> 101
> 5.292
> 474
> 119
> 79
> 151

NGO to exert pressure on the company to discontinue plans to locate a salt factory at a whale reproduction site.

Most ethical investments so far have been made in the United States, where one eighth of total investment funds are committed to responsible investment (i.e. 2,350 billion dollars). But this type of investment is rapidly increasing in Europe. Responsible investment amounts to around 3,000 billion dollars worldwide.

Economic indicators are also encouraging

Naturally, the major international corporate groups claim to be committed to sustainable development. Too often sustainable development in this context is perceived only in its environmental aspects (biodiversity must be conserved, but cultural and economic di-versity also need to be protected). Some leaders have understood, either through conviction or in anticipation of socio-economic demand, that respect for the principles of sustainable development is a precondition for continuing their

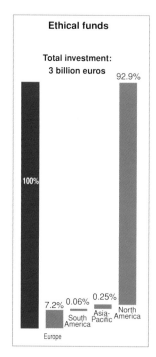

Ethical funds

Total investment: 3 billion euros

92.9%

100%

7.2% 0.06% 0.25%

South America Asia-Pacific North America

Europe

business activities. Through the combined effects of increasing regulation, public and financial sector pressures, and the series of recent industrial and social disasters and financial scandals, a growing number of companies publish annual sustainable development reports. Using widely comprehensible indices, such reports present objectives and evaluate company performance with respect to, for example, environmental impacts (air, water, soil, climate), accidents, corruption and solidarity. Greater transparency is a sign of progress, but it is the vigilance of shareholders, investors and consumers that makes the difference between declared good intentions and responsible management.

It's up to consumers to become involved.

Consumers can contribute to sustainable development, especially by supporting more equitable trade relations with developing countries. Equitable commerce is aimed at ensuring decent revenues for producers and their families (especially through reducing the number of intermediaries) and encourages them to adopt environmentally friendly production methods. In 2001, European companies participating in equitable commerce imported cocoa from 50,000 South American and African producers - an alternative to a system of international trade carried out solely according to the laws of the primary raw materials market. The European Association for Equitable Commerce imports from 45 Southern countries, allowing 800,000 families (about 5 million people) to live decently from their own production.

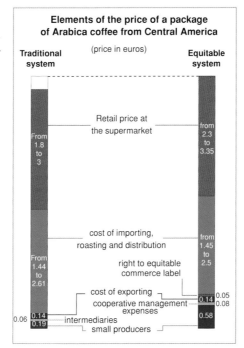

Elements of the price of a package of Arabica coffee from Central America

(price in euros)

Traditional system

Equitable system

Retail price at the supermarket — From 1.8 to 3 — from 2.3 to 3.35

cost of importing, roasting and distribution — From 1.44 to 2.61 — from 1.45 to 2.5

right to equitable commerce label

cost of exporting — 0.14 — 0.05 / 0.08
cooperative management expenses — 0.58
intermediaries — 0.06 / 0.14 / 0.19
small producers

We live in an extremely complicated period of uncertainty and interdependency, with its complex ecological systems, globalization of information dissemination, dramatic changes in power and knowledge, and increased risks.

The political and economic worlds cannot operate on their own. Civil society, confronted by technological, nutritional, health, economic and social risks, is no longer content to be excluded from decision-making that affects its future and that of its children. The dominant development model of the last 40 years has had boomerang effects that cannot be combatted without the participation of every part of society.

Sustainable development leads to a new way of exercising authority, based on real acceptance of responsibilities and the recognition of complementary cultures, know-how and approaches. It relies on strong commitments and the use of considerable resources, associating governments, civil society and international institutions endowed with powers of arbitration and coercion. Based on values supported by a growing share of the population, guiding principles for action are being established. The way is being prepared for development that is better controlled, characterized by solidarity, and literally "sustainable" – this is the only way out of the present environmental and social crisis. Sustainable development is a social contract for the planet, which should be signed and put into effect without further delay.

Important dates from 1992 to 2002

Source: Le Monde

1992

Environment
170 heads of state and government at Rio conference on environment and development adopt Agenda 21, an action programme for sustainable development in the 21st century. Agenda 21 sets out 27 principles and integrates over 2,500 recommendations. Conventions on climate change, biological diversity and desertification also agreed, as well as a declaration on sustainable forest management.

Peace
Nobel Peace Prize awarded to Rigoberta Menchu, symbol of resistance by indigenous peoples.

Human Rights
Just before Rio Earth Summit, indigenous peoples organize their first world conference on territory, environment and development.

1993

Environment
Century's worst river flooding in the United States causes 40 deaths and estimated 10 billion dollars in damage.
Earthquake in India kills 30,000 people.
London Convention bans dumping of industrial and radioactive waste at sea.

Peace
130 countries sign treaty banning use and production of chemical weapons.
United Kingdom and Russia agree to suspend nuclear testing.
Nobel Peace Prize awarded jointly to Nelson Mandela and Frederik de Klerk. South African Parliament ends apartheid.

Ethics
In Italy the "clean hands" investigation of corruption targets over 150 politicians.

1994

Environment
Meeting of 30 Mediterranean countries at Tunis adopts an Agenda 21 and creates Mediterranean Commission on Sustainable Development.
Basel Convention bans hazardous waste exports by OECD countries.

Peace
Rwanda: 500,000 deaths and 2 million refugees.
Nobel Peace Prize awarded jointly to Itzhak Rabin, Shimon Peres and Yasser Arafat.

Human Rights
182 countries participate in Cairo population conference. Abortion rights and rights of women at centre of discussions.

1995

Environment
Earthquake in Japan kills over 5,000 people.
In the Netherlands flooding results in evacuation of 200,000 people.

Peace
Japan: chemical weapon attack kills 10 people and poisons 5,000
South Africa: capital punishment abolished.
Nobel Peace Prize awarded to British anti-nuclear activist Joseph Rotblat and his movement, Pugwash.

Human Rights
181 countries and 20,000 NGOs participate in Peking conference on women's rights.

Solidarity
At Copenhagen summit on social development heads of state and government make commitment to struggle against exclusion.

1996

Environment
Participants in "city summit" at Istanbul agree on need to take integrated and participatory actions to make cities safer, healthier and fairer. Right to housing recognized as integral to human rights as a whole.
Convention on desertification comes into force.

Peace
Nobel Peace Prize awarded to Monsignor Carlos Felipe Ximes Belo and José Ramos-Horta, spokesmen for East Timor.

Human Rights
Rome summit on world food adopts declaration reaffirming right of each human being not to suffer from hunger.

1997

Environment
Iran: earthquake kills 1,613 and injures 3,712.
Central Europe: Flooding of Oder River causes 115 deaths, with over 150,000 evacuated.
Europe: after several months' inquiry, the European Parliament acts to control "mad cow disease".
At Kyoto conference on climate change 159 countries agree on 5.2% reduction of greenhouse gas emissions by 2010 compared with 1990 levels.

Peace
United States Senate ratifies international convention banning chemical weapons.
121 countries sign Ottawa treaty banning antipersonnel mines. The United States, Russia and China refuse to sign.
The Nobel Peace Prize awarded to the campagne for the prohibition of antipersonnal mines.

Human Rights
Oslo conference on child labour adopts action programme aimed at abolishing child labour within 15 years.

1998

Environment
Hurricane Mitch devastates Central America (12,000 dead, 13,000 missing and millions of victims).
Afghanistan: two large-scale earthquakes kill nearly 10,000 people and destroy dozens of villages.
China: floods cause over 3,000 deaths.
France: international conference on water and sustainable development.

Peace
Russia: Alexandre Nikitine, who revealed radioactive pollution by Russian navy, tried for "high treason" away from the public eye.
120 countries agree to create international criminal court to judge

and prevent (through dissuasion) war crimes, crimes against humanity and genocide. The United States is one of seven countries voting against it.

Solidarity
Nobel Prize for Economies awarded to Indian economist Amartya Sen, specialist in poverty.

1999

Environment
Environmental impact of depleted uranium used during the Kosovo conflict: for the first time the United Nations Environment Programme directs the inquiry.
Turkey: earthquake and refinery fire in the Izmit region, killing almost 15,000 people and leaving 25,000 wounded and 200,000 homeless.
Europe: unprecedented storms destroy thousands of hectares of forest; 60 French regions declared disaster areas.
Japan: radioactive leak in northwestern Tokyo (the country's seventh nuclear accident and worst since 1995).

Peace
UN Security Council condemns use of child soldiers, estimated to number 300,000.
Kosovo conflict: over 80,000 refugees.
East Timor conflict: some 140,000 refugees.
Nobel Peace Prize awarded to Médecins sans Frontières, French organisation created in 1971.

Citizenship
Demonstrations against existing international trade regulations at WTO meeting in Seattle involving 135 countries.

Human rights
Canada: creation of Nunavut ("our land") government in Inuit territory.

Ethics
Over 200,000 Rumanians take part in "marches of despair" against political corruption.
United States: Monsanto begins commercialization of cereals whose seeds have been sterilized though genetic modification.
Europe: food crises, including "mad cow disease", poisoning of chickens and contamination of pork by dioxin.

2000

Environment
14 years after one of its reactors exploded, Chernobyl nuclear installation definitively closes; Belorussian Professor Yuri Bandzhevsky remains imprisoned for drawing attention to health impacts of the Chernobyl disaster.
European transport ministers agree to reinforce maritime security and responsibility of companies charged with verifying tanker safety, in an effort to prevent oil spills.
At Johannesburg 120 countries acknowledge precautionary principle with respect to toxic substances.

Peace
United States: a million women demonstrate against firearms lobby.
Russia: Duma ratifies treaty banning nuclear testing.
Fourth Euro-Mediterranean Conference in Marseilles (France) supports creation of sovereign Palestinian state.

Nobel Peace Prize awarded to South Korean President Kim Dae-Jung for his work aimed at reconciliation with North Korea.

Human rights
Chinese dissident Gao Xing-jian, a refugee in France since 1988, receives Nobel prize for Literature.

Solidarity
First European-African summit in Cairo dominated by issue of African debt (350 billion dollars).
Over 160 heads of state and government attending "millennium summit" confirm their commitment to struggle against poverty; Rio engagements reconfirmed.

Ethics
Council of Europe announces opposition to human gene patenting.
138 countries in Montreal adopt protocol on biosecurity authorizing countries to ban GM imports.
OECD publishes black list of 15 countries accused of money laundering (including Liechtenstein, Israel, Lebanon, Russia).
At IMF and World Bank meeting, and in the presence of thousands of demonstrators, 182 countries address lack of transparency.

2001

Environment
Earthquake in India kills 30,000.
100 countries sign Stockholm convention banning 12 toxic substances (POPs, or persistent organic pollutants).
Despite the United States' refusal to participate, 164 countries agree on methods of applying the Kyoto Protocol to the Climate Convention.

Peace
Fifth conference on bacteriological weapons ends in failure as United States opposes any system of control.
During UN conference on light weapons the United States, Russia and China block negotiations on reduction and trafficking of these weapons.
Nobel peace prize awarded to UN and its Secretary-General, Kofi Annan, who is reelected for five years.

Human Rights
France is 12th country to ratify treaty on International Criminal Court, which will address genocide, war crimes and crimes against humanity (in 2002 this treaty was ratified by 60 countries).
Middle East conflict paralyses negotiations at third United Nations conference on racism, xenophobia and racial discrimination. The 160 countries present express their apprehension about fate of the Palestinians. Final report qualifies slavery as crime against humanity.
In Afghanistan head of Taliban regime orders destruction of giant 5th century Buddhas at Bamiyan.

Citizenship
Thousands of NGOs at first global social forum in Porto Alegre, Brazil, demand participation of civil society in international trade.

Solidarity
UN conference on AIDS creates global AIDS and health fund.

Ethics
International pharmaceutical industry abandons legal proceedings against South African government for distributing generic drugs to fight AIDS.

Index

Bibliography

Les Nouveaux Utopistes du développement durable — Anne-Marie DUCROUX – Éditions Autrement, 2002

Le Développement durable : dynamique et constitution d'un projet — E. ZACCAI – Éditions Éco polis, 2002

Ressources mondiales – Les hommes et les écosystèmes — WRI, Banque mondiale, PNUD et PNUE, Éditions Eska, 2001

Risk Society — Ulrich BECK – Sage Publications Ltd, 1992

Where on earth are we going — Maurice STRONG – Montréal – Texere Publishing, 2001

La Biosphère, notre Terre vivante — Jean-Paul DELEAGE – Éditions Gallimard, 2001

Repenser l'inégalité — Amartya SEN – Éditions du Seuil, 2000

Le viol de la Terre : depuis des siècles, toutes les civilisations sont coupables — C. PONTING – Éditions du NIL, 2000

La Fin du développement – Naissance d'une alternative ? — François PARTANT – Éditions Actes Sud, 1997

L'Économique et le vivant — René PASSET – Éditions Economica, 1996

La planète Terre entre nos mains Serge ANTOINE, Martine BARRÈRE, Geneviève VERBRUGGE, La Documentation Française, 1994

L'Éco-développement — Ignacy SACHS – Éditions Syros, 1993

Terre-Patrie — Edgar MORIN, Anne-Brigitte KERN – Éditions du Seuil, 1993

Le principe de responsabilité, une éthique pour la civilisation technologique — Hans JONAS – Éditions du Cerf, 1993

Web Sites

www.comite21.org
www.unep.org
www.undp.org
www.wri.org
www.iucn.org
www.eea.eu.int
www.transparency.org

www.rsf.fr
www.amnesty.asso.fr/
www.fidh.org
www.uneptie.org
www.ifen.fr
www.clcv.org
www.wbcsd.ch

www.developpement-local.com/
www.coordinationsud.org/
www.agora21.org
www.wwf.fr
www.planetecologie.org
www.sommetjohannesburg.org